GOTHIC CONTEMPORARIES

SERIES PREFACE

Gothic Literary Studies is dedicated to publishing groundbreaking scholarship on Gothic in literature and film.The Gothic,which has been subjected to a variety of critical and theoretical approaches, is a form which plays an important role in our understanding of literary, intellectual and cultural histories. The series seeks to promote challenging and innovative approaches to Gothic which question any aspect of the Gothic tradition or perceived critical orthodoxy. Volumes in the series explore how issues such as gender, religion, nation and sexuality have shaped our view of the Gothic tradition . Both academically rigorous and informed by the latest developments in critical theory, the series provides an important focus for scholastic developments in Gothic studies, literary studies, cultural studies and critical theory.The series will be of interest to students of all levels and to scholars and teachers of the Gothic and literary and cultural histories.

SERIES EDITORS

EDITORIAL BOARD

Gothic Contemporaries
The Haunted Text

Joanne Watkiss

UNIVERSITY OF WALES PRESS
CARDIFF
2012

www.uwp.co.uk

British Library CIP Data
A catalogue record for this book is available from the British Library.

ISBN   978-0-7083-2455-4 (hardback)
           978-0-7083-2456-1 (paperback)
e-ISBN 978-0-7083-2457-8

Typeset in Wales by Eira Fenn Gaunt, Cardiff
Printed by CPI Antony Rowe, Chippenham, Wiltshire

CONTENTS

Acknowledgements

Thanks are owed to Dr Sue Chaplin and Dr Nicholas Cox from the School of Cultural Studies at Leeds Metropolitan University. I am also indebted to my parents for their support.

Conference papers based on chapters 1, 2 and 5 were presented at a variety of international conferences: "'I'll take the ghost's word for a thousand pound": Bret Easton Ellis's *Lunar Park*' was presented at the International Gothic conference (Aix-en-Provence) in June 2007 and at the 'Legacies' conference (Zürich) in September of the same year. "'Building, dwelling, writing": Mark Z. Danielewski's *House of Leaves*' was presented at 'The Novel and its Borders' conference (Aberdeen) in July 2008 and at the 'Uncanny Media' conference (Utrecht) in August 2008. 'Catastrophe, travel and the letter: *The Story of Lucy Gault*' was presented at the 'Derrida Today' conference (London) in July 2010. An earlier version of chapter 3, 'Ghosts in the head: mourning, memory and Derridean "trace" in John Banville's *The Sea*', was published in the *Irish Journal of Gothic and Horror Studies* in March 2007, just as a previous draft of chapter 5, 'The horror of inheritance: poisonous lineage in Bret Easton Ellis's *Lunar Park*', was published in the *Horror Studies* journal by Intellect Books in December 2010. I am grateful to the editors of these journals for their permission to use the material in this book.

Acknowledgements

Extracts from *The Sea* by John Banville, copyright © 2005 by John Banville, reproduced by permission of Macmillan Publishers (UK and Commonwealth) and of Alfred A. Knopf, a division of Random House, Inc. (world).

Extracts from *The Gathering* by Anne Enright, copyright © 2007 by Anne Enright, reproduced by permission of the author and of the Random House Group Ltd (UK and Commonwealth).

Extracts from *Lunar Park* by Bret Easton Ellis, copyright © 2005 by Bret Easton Ellis, reproduced by permission of International Creative Management, Inc. (UK) and of Alfred A. Knopf, a division of Random House, Inc. (US and Canada).

Extracts from *Beyond Black* by Hilary Mantel, copyright © 2005 by Hilary Mantel, reproduced by permission of A. M. Heath & Co. Ltd (world).

For the other J. Watkiss

Introduction.

The Horror of Failed Exchanges: Signification, Communication, Ethics, Death, Inheritance and Currency

∽

A rather astute student once said to me: 'is there such a thing as the contemporary Gothic?' I hesitated before I answered, because I realized this was an impossible question to answer. For starters, there is no such thing, entity or body of work delineated as the contemporary Gothic. So his question raised all kinds of other interesting questions: was there such a thing as the Gothic in the first place? If so, where and when was the Gothic? Has it been and gone? Can it be located within a specific time frame? Impossible. How can limits be placed upon concepts that frustrate those very limits? As David Punter has written, 'Gothic writing is a contested site'.[1] So perhaps the Gothic has never existed as such: instead, what we might consider as Gothic is that which insists on remaining, that which persists as a haunting trace and refuses to be exorcized. So the question my student really asked was: how do we study a set of ideas that frustrate the very language used to articulate them? My convoluted answer (by which time he wished he hadn't asked) was that the Gothic has never been a genre to define. This is certainly the current critical consensus – a move, as outlined by Catherine Spooner, 'towards understanding Gothic as a set of discourses rather than simply as a genre'.[2] Therefore, the contemporary Gothic can be understood through its echoing of concepts and ideas that have been around for centuries. Pre-Walpole, and even pre-Shakespeare, there are themes under exploration that have been aligned with the Gothic. As Alex Warwick has acknowledged the 'defining characteristics [of the Gothic] are its mobility and continued capacity for reinvention'.[3] Therefore, *Gothic Contemporaries* explores twenty-first-century responses to these concepts which are simultaneously new and old (hence the endless plagiarism and uncanny repetition for which the Gothic is well known). In this book, the term 'contemporaries' refers to concepts explored in the texts under discussion here, and not the authors themselves. These concepts are signification, communication, ethics, death, inheritance and currency; all of these should give rise to an exchange of some kind, but as these texts demonstrate, such interactions are fraught with failure. These key themes are examined across six novels which are haunted by the exploration of similar concepts within discourses of law, philosophy and psychoanalysis as well as within other literary texts. Hence, these texts are haunted by other texts through a series of uncanny inheritances that simultaneously renew the concepts afresh. The books reveal silences, gaps, miscommunication, absences and contradictions that threaten their sense of book-as-totality while permitting space for productive discussion. This book is a celebration of the productivity of such liminal spaces.

The themes under discussion here are also the focus for Derrida's later works in particular. As Jodey Castricano has written,[4] it is tempting to refer to Derrida as a Gothic novelist as the themes he repeatedly returns to have been aligned with the Gothic. As Nicholas Royle points out, 'Derrida's work throws new light, patterns and shadows on "the Gothic"'.[5] His discussion of ghosts in *Specters of Marx: The State of the Debt, the Work of Mourning, and the New International*[6] initiated a renewed theoretical approach to haunting. Other key Derridean works explored here are *The Post Card: From Socrates to Freud and Beyond*,[7] *The Gift of Death*,[8] *Of Hospitality*[9] and *Paper Machine*.[10] Earlier texts such as *Dissemination*,[11] *Of Grammatology*[12] and *Margins of Philosophy*[13] are also discussed in this book, although less frequently than Derrida's later texts. Other theoretical works explored here are Sigmund Freud's essay 'The uncanny'[14] and his discussion of the archive which underpins *Archive Fever: A Freudian Impression*; Julia Kristeva's analysis of abjection in her essay 'Powers of horror' and mourning in *Black Sun*;[15] Emmanuel Levinas's discourse on ethics as outlined in *Totality and Infinity*[16] and Mark Wigley's *The Architecture of Deconstruction: Derrida's Haunt*.[17] Other literary critics whose ideas permeate this book are Peter Goodrich and his discussion of the law in *Oedipus Lex: Psychoanalysis, History, Law*;[18] Gideon Ofrat's *The Jewish Derrida*;[19] Julian Wolfreys's discussion of the Gothic and textuality in *Victorian Hauntings: Spectrality, Gothic, the Uncanny and Literature*;[20] Anne Williams's *Art of Darkness*[21] and Carolyn Steedman's discussion of dust and the archive. Hence, this book explores a set of concepts whose intertextual references range from Shakespeare to Bret Easton Ellis, and from Horace Walpole to Derrida. As such, this study is less interested in historical limits, preferring to relish the chaotic creativity of intertextuality and uncanny repetition. Despite the fact that the texts under discussion in this book (novels, theory and criticism[22]) have been published since the year 2000, themes covered here are just as relevant to the seventeenth century as they are to the twenty-first.

In its exploration of concepts aligned with the Gothic, this book gestures towards texts which might be referred to as 'classics', such as *The Castle of Otranto*.[23] However, as this study will demonstrate, such a text can be considered contemporary through its conceptual concerns, despite being published in 1764. For instance, *The Castle of Otranto* concludes with an ending that might initially appear conservative, as a threat is raised and subsequently neutralized. However, once boundaries (typically legal or moral) have been tested, they cannot be reinstated. So although Dracula is staked through the heart, and the Castle of Otranto is returned to its rightful owner, things can never be the same again. There is no going back: the threat continues just as the themes of *The Castle of Otranto* persistently haunt texts published much later.

The first concept under discussion is the process of reading which is the focus for chapter 1: 'H(a)unting the House: Consuming Mark Z. Danielewski's *House of Leaves*'. Considered as a quest for signification, the act of reading is read as a violent, consuming process. Mirroring the critics' search for a hidden meaning that will explain the text, the protagonist of *House of Leaves* explores a space that, I will argue, is the virtual space of a book. Through multiple references to hunting, this chapter explores the violence of a reading that attempts to restrict a text's plurality. Therefore, *House of Leaves* suggests a disseminative experience of reading as explored in Derrida's essay 'Dissemination'.[24] Reading as hunting results in a text haunted by its own plurality; a dissemination that ensures there can be no arrival at a transcendental signified. Like a maze with no centre, such an experience leads to unutterable horror, as endless repetitions and echoes promise arrival but never deliver. Such plurality fails to reaffirm the totality of the text, and so reading becomes a practice of horror as the network of associations that constitute language becomes a maze in which the reader, like the protagonist, gets lost.

Through a misinterpreted child suicide, the horror of the unspeakable also relates to chapter 2: 'The Horror of Miscommunication: *The Story of Lucy Gault*'. Focusing on the detrimental effects of miscommunication, this chapter expands on the non-arrival at signification foregrounded in chapter 1. Just as the exchange of reading demands meaning, the attempt to communicate demands understanding, and the process of letter-sending requires an arrival and a response. Like Derrida's *The Post Card: From Socrates to Freud and Beyond*, *The Story of Lucy Gault* is concerned with the consequences of failed communication. Through accident, misinterpretation and censorship, the attempt to communicate effectively is fraught with inaccuracies. This becomes evident when a missing child is thought to have committed suicide, and life becomes death. Although alive, the child is positioned as a monstrosity by those around her who are fearful of the horrific event that comes to determine her. Isolated and outcast, she becomes, like Frankenstein, a victim of misinterpretation and censorship.

Child suicide is also explored in chapter 3: 'The Gothic Double Revised: Memory, Mourning and Illegal Twins in *The Sea*'. Through the illegal implications of incest between twins, the boundary of self and other is interrogated. Such a secret results in child suicide, an event that horrifies and haunts the memory of the protagonist who is mourning their deaths as well as his wife's recent passing. Through the mourning process, an understanding of ethical relations with others can be achieved. As explored through Emmanuel Levinas's *Totality and Infinity: An Essay on Exteriority*, mourning highlights a dependence on others for stability and reassurance. When those others are deceased, the mourner becomes fragmented and his sense of self divided, an experience which horrifies the mourner into believing that he too is dead. As relations with others have been understood as a mutual exchange of give and take, this chapter suggests this process is a fraught one that ensures the stability of the self rather than a relationship that is mutually beneficial. Through the spectrality of memory, the mind is explored as a Gothic space or, as Derrida suggests in 'The double session',[25] a 'double stage' that operates in the past and present simultaneously.

Chapter 4, 'Conjuration, Digestion, Expulsion: The Law of Mourning in *The Gathering*', interrogates the tradition of mourning as a Gothic practice. In Anne Enright's text, the protagonist mourns her brother, whose corpse is simultaneously welcomed to 'lie in state' and then banished. His ghost, however, is not welcomed and therefore cannot be evicted. As an event that demands an exchange, mourning is understood as a process that attempts to evict the body and soul of the deceased. In this chapter, this is understood as a legal require-ment, as instigated by the law's involvement in death through paper documentation. Such association frustrates legal boundaries to expose a reliance on thresholds that are unstable. By permitting a corpse entry to the home, the law of mourning ensures a digestive response as the deceased are conjured, consumed and then expelled. Such a guest highlights the uncanniness of the home and the hospitality of its boundaries as explored through Derrida's *Of Hospitality*. This threshold anxiety becomes more acute when the guest is a spectre, parasitical rather than welcomed. The ghost refuses the law's process of exchange, undermining the boundaries of the law and the home. Such exposure results in a horror of realization. As Derrida's essays 'Before the law'[26] and 'Force of law: the mystical foundation of authority'[27] suggest, the law depends on insecure boundaries to construct a façade of security.

The law of the father is the focus for chapter 5: 'An Inherited Poison: *Hamlet*, *The Castle of Otranto* and *Lunar Park*'. As explored through the exchange of inheritance, death ensures repeated obedience to the will of the deceased father. As depicted in *Hamlet*, *The Castle of Otranto* and *Lunar Park*, the ghost of the patriarch appears in order to correct an incorrect lineage. However, through such apparitions, the role of the father is undermined: once boundaries are unsettled, the threat persists as a time out of joint cannot be set right by spectral intervention. Instead, things are only set further out of joint, as the law's reliance on the supernatural exposes its inability to guard its own boundaries. Therefore, as explored in *Specters of Marx*, the horror of inheritance is apparent as lineage is poisoned by the very attempt to reassert it. By following the word of the father, the son must act illegally, resulting in madness and halted lineage. The role of lineage can be understood through the *pharmakon*.[28] As both medicine and poison, the *pharmakon* demonstrates the contradictory nature of inheritance which simultaneously attempts to correct lineage and dislocate it. As this chapter suggests, inheritance is bound by blood, a fluid which acts as both cure and poison to the problems of inheritance. In this way, *Lunar Park* suggests a poisonous lineage where the word of the father (and of tradition) must be questioned.

The sixth and final chapter, 'Gothic Currency: Mortgage, Debt and Exchange in *Beyond Black*', explores the relationship between the law, finance and textual ownership. As the protagonist of this text is a psychic, she is persistently haunted by the ghosts of her past. Through their concern with space, location and debt, ghosts in *Beyond Black* remain bound to the long arm of the law. Through the contractual pledge of the mortgage, both the living and the dead are chained to space through a continuous debt. As a weight that haunts and horrifies the homeowner, the law is explored as a spectral presence. The space of the home places its inhabitants under house arrest, an uncanny binding which challenges the home as sanctuary. Like the ghost and the sign, currency substitutes itself for the variable value it signifies, emphasizing the uncanniness of the homely, as explored in Derrida's *Given Time: Counterfeit Money*[29] and *Specters of Marx*.

1

H(a)unting the House: Consuming Mark Z. Danielewski's House of Leaves

&

House of Leaves is an observational sketch on a film, paradoxically written by a blind man named Zampanò. Zampanò includes photographs, interviews, monologues and comments from critics, theorists, scholars and psychiatrists as part of his narrative. Described as 'endless snarls of words ... on old napkins, the tattered edges of an envelope, once even on the back of a postage stamp',[1] this fragmentary account of a film is based on the Navidson family: Will,[2] his partner Karen, his twin brother Tom and their children Daisy and Chad. The film documents their move to a new home where a 'dark doorless hallway appear[s] out of nowhere in the west wall'.[3] This space is then subject to rigorous explorations by Navidson and many others who desire not only to colonize it but to define it. As an abyssal realm uninhabitable because of its impenetrable darkness and extreme cold, the hallway refuses to be contained and ultimately consumes those who attempt to force it to signify.

This chapter will argue that Danielewski's hallway presents the reader with the experience of reading. Although much has been said in relation to the textual architecture of this novel indicating that the text itself is presented as a house, this chapter will suggest that the abyssal hallway is a book. Instead of an uncanny addition to his home in the shape of a hallway, Navidson's discovery is a book. The ensuing explorations[4] of the hallway depict his multiple efforts to read the book: the corridors he follows are the pathways of associations between signifiers that endlessly defer their signified. His reading, however, is not passive. Instead, Navidson reads violently, obsessed with interpreting and tracking down a transcendental signified to such an extent that he consumes the text. In turn, the horror of the unreadable book exerts its own power to consume, inducing physical and mental afflictions in its readers. Through his frustrations, Navidson leads himself down several pathways, each one repeating the one before it. The exploration of the hallway space represents the wandering eye of the reader who attempts to decipher the meaning of a text. Instead of arriving at the centre of the maze clear of the text's meaning, Navidson endlessly reads and rereads the book, his eyes following the multiple disseminations associated with all signifiers. Through repetition and infinite deferral, the maze of language that he enters refuses to be deciphered. As a result, his violence increases to such an extent that he burns the text to ash, and hence the haunted text becomes the hunted text. In doing so, he realizes the futility of interpretation and the totality of the book, and is forced to appreciate the plurality of the signifier. As a text that refutes its own signification, *House of Leaves* links its reader with the protagonist reader as Navidson mirrors the critic's quest for signification. Danielewski's writing is a game that encourages the reader to search for a meaning cryptically concealed, only to find, like Navidson, that there is only multiplicity. Just like language, the novel encourages an endless wandering without arrival, an experience that is both valuable and enjoyable.

Navidson's repeated attempts to enter and explore the book are supplemented by the narrator, Zampanò, and his inclusion of multiple viewpoints offered by both fictional and non-fictional figures. Zampanò includes several references and quotations from other texts in an attempt to interpret Navidson's reading. His intertextual references are extremely playful as he refers to non-fictional figures and fictionalizes their contribution to *House of Leaves* whilst also referring to fictional characters as real individuals. Navidson's journey of interpretation is repeatedly interrupted by critics, theorists and scholars attempting to interpret his interpretation. This results in a novel of quotation from multiple contributors, echoing Navidson's own experience of reading as dissemination. Hence, Danielewski's text offers repeated attempts to interpret Navidson's attempt to interpret a book. Furthermore, his reading is assisted by several editorial voices[5] that highlight the allusions of specific signifiers. For instance, one narrative voice of *The Navidson Record* considers that 'the implication in "abort" is the failure to attain a goal' (p. 124). As a labyrinthine web of associations, *House of Leaves* repeatedly defers the reader and the protagonist beyond the space of the text. As Derrida writes, 'repetition is the very movement of non-truth: the presence of what gets lost, disperses itself, multiplies itself through mimemes, icons, phantasms, simulacra, etc.'[6] Combined with my own attempts to interpret the novel (although not for the transcendental signified that Navidson so desperately seeks), the reader is caught in a web of textual pathways that leads neither from an origin nor to a destination. These repetitions constitute the dissemination that Navidson experiences within the book, as the desire to deduce the text results in further interpretations. In this way, Danielewski is commenting on textual analysis as a process of multiplicity. Such multiplicity is echoed in 'Plato's pharmacy':

> In the enclosed space of the pharmacy, the reverberations of the mono-logue are immeasurably amplified. The walled-in voice strikes against the rafters, the words come apart, bits and pieces of sentences are separated, disarticulated parts begin to circulate through the corridors, become fixed for a round or two, translate each other, become rejoined, bounce off each other, contradict each other, make trouble, tell on each other, come back like answers, organise their exchanges, protect each other, institute an internal commerce, take themselves for a dialogue.[7]

As Derrida suggests, textual analysis constitutes endless exchanges that result in a chaotic web of associations. Under duress, like the 'walled-in voice', words become energized, resulting in both fragmentation and rearrangement. Because Navidson chooses to read his text violently, he provides the energy for explosive signification: the more he attempts to capture the text, the more frenzied his reading becomes. In reference to *House of Leaves*, Catherine Spooner writes that 'it is difficult to analyse the book without merely repeating what is already within it'.[8] As such, Danielewski's text has been carefully constructed to ensure that (like Navidson's book) it un-cannily repeats itself. Instances of repetition in *House of Leaves* are evident as Navidson continually tries to enter the book, reading deeper and deeper each time. After his own readings fail to penetrate the meaning of the text, Navidson turns to several others to aid his interpretation including a team of explorers, Holloway, Jed and Wax. As is evidenced through the subheadings (Exploration A, Navidson's first attempt to read alone; Explorations 1–3, the repeated attempts of the team; Exploration 4, Holloway's descent into madness, and Exploration 5 where Navidson attempts a final reading), the disseminative experience of the book is echoed through the team's and Navidson's journeys of reading.

On his first reading, Navidson finds himself in a dark, cold corridor comprising a 'constant stream of corners and walls all of them unreadable and perfectly smooth' (p. 64). His first observation posits the book as 'unreadable' and extremely repetitive in its 'replicating chambers and corridors' (p. 90). As an experience of reading, Navidson's wandering from corridor to corridor suggests persistent movement instigated by the signifiers he encounters: 'Navidson pushes ahead, moving deeper and deeper into the house, eventually passing a number of doorways leading off into alternate passageways or chambers' (p. 64). As is the case in many of Derrida's works, spatial metaphors such as the pathway are aligned with the experience of reading: 'we will be able neither to do without the passage through a written text, nor to avoid the order of the disorder produced within it.'[9] Therefore, Navidson's endless wandering is an experience of reading aligned with Derrida's concept of dissemination or 'the detour of the sign'.[10] The arbitrary relationship between signifier and signified ensures that meaning depends on difference as a signifier is related to its signified through multiple associations (and differences) with other signifiers. As the translator's introduction to *Dissemination* suggests, 'language as such is already constituted by the very distances and differences it seeks to overcome'.[11] The endless allusions associated with each signifier constitute what Derrida refers to as iterability or citationality. Therefore, instead of one signifier relating to one signified, each signifier refers to several other signifiers, a dispersal known as dissemination. 'Essentially and lawfully, every concept is inscribed in a chain or in a system within which it refers to the other, to other concepts, by means of a systematic play of differences.'[12] The multiple trajectories associated with each signifier result in an endless echoing of terms which lead down several different pathways. Derrida's ideas on dissemination refer back to Saussure's affirmation that 'a word can always evoke everything that can be associated with it in one way or another . . . a particular word is like the center of a constellation; it is the point of convergence of an indefinite number of co-ordinated terms'.[13] Like a constellation of stars, one signifier can relate to several others resulting in an increasingly wide array of signifieds. Navidson's experience of reading echoes the plurality of the signifier as he wanders through the multiple associations of each word he encounters as 'an incredibly complex and frequently disorienting series of turns' (p. 68). The words direct his reading through endless pathways that refute any central meaning in the text, initiating 'convolution, interference, confusion, and even decentric ideas on design and construction . . . empty rooms, long hallways and dead ends' (p. 109). In addition to the meandering structures that Navidson must navigate through, the space of the book periodically changes shape. By placing a penny on the floor, Navidson attempts to mark the space so that he can clearly locate his position. However, he 'immediately sees how drastically everything has changed', and 'the penny he left behind, which should have been at least a hundred feet further, lies directly before him' (p. 68). The space of the book has shrunk to bring his marker closer. Members of the exploratory team also note 'how all the walls have shifted' (p. 84), as repetitive deferrals constantly reorganize the space of the book.

The efforts of those that read the text are focused on finding 'something defining, or at least some kind of indication of an outsideness to that place' (p. 119). Without an outside, there is no end to the structures that surround them, inducing a mania akin to the experience of a maze. The repetitive space of the book gestures towards a 'doorway leading to another hallway spawning yet another endless series of empty rooms and passageways, all with walls potentially hiding and thus hinting at a possible exterior, though invariably winding up as just another border to another interior' (p. 119). There is therefore no clear exit to the book, which refutes the team's mastery over it. As such, the team approach the text aggressively, determined to decipher its meaning: 'Navidson and Tom are classic hunters. They select weapons (tools: reason) and they track their prey (a solution)' (p. 37). The association of weaponry with reading indicates their violent approach to the text as reading is aligned with tracking prey.

Like hunting, their approach to the text is to follow the signs of a path clearly indicated for them to reach their central goal, the prey or the cryptically concealed meaning of the text.

Such a trail will be achieved by following the associations between signifiers. The fact that there is something to be found in the book is not doubted, as suggested by the team's logocentric tool of reason.[14] A multitude of possibilities is presented to the team, including that the book 'conceals a secret? Protects something? Imprisons or hides some kind of monster? Or, for that matter, imprisons or hides an innocent? As the Holloway team soon discover, answers to these questions are not exactly forthcoming' (p. 111). The hunt for prey is the quest for a transcendental signified that will ground the other signifiers towards one united meaning; a signification that will cure the horror of the unreadable text, ensuring that the multiplicity of endless pathways is mastered and mapped. Only then will they locate the outside of the text, the limit to which an arrival can be announced and celebrated.

While inside the book, they begin to hear a loud noise: 'Navidson freezes, unsure whether or not he really just heard something growl' (p. 67). The source of the growl is never found although the team assume the sound emanates from the desired prey. The animalistic associations of the growl suggest that the members of the team are no longer the hunters but are now the hunted. As Wax asks, '"what if that sound's not from the wall's shifting but coming from something else, some kind of thing?"' (p. 95). Such a noise suggests the absent presence of the transcendental signified: 'soon enough they all begin to detect that inimitable growl, like calving glaciers, far off in the distance' (p. 123). Aligned with the collapse of sheets of ice, the noise relates to the disintegration of colossal structures, an indication of the fragility of meaning. The mysterious source of the sound is increasingly translated as threatening, simultaneously nearby and far away: a '"heaviness" which always seemed to be crouching, ready to spring, just a few feet away' (p. 118). Such a reference posits the transcendental signified as a source of fear that is not seen; like a Gothic monster, the growl is aligned with the experience of terror. As a sound that cannot be located, the noise produces a psychological response akin to the anticipation of the supernatural in the Gothic, an expectation that usually does not arrive. As a spectral presence, the transcendental signified 'reserv[es] itself, not exposing itself, in regular fashion it exceeds the order of truth at a certain precise point . . . in every exposition it would be exposed to disappearing as disappearance. It would risk appearing: disappearing.'[15]

After following the growl for days, the members of Holloway's team become increasingly sceptical that the prey they seek will be found. As the promise of a transcendental signified, the growl offers the possibility of arrival. However, as the suggestion of a source which never arrives, the growl is repeatedly deferred: 'the faint growl returns, rolling through the darkness like thunder' (p. 68). As Derrida suggests in 'Différance', the arrival at signification is aligned with a present absence.

> When we cannot grasp or show the thing, state the present, the being-present, when the present cannot be presented, we signify, we go through the detour of the sign. We take or give signs. We signal. The sign, in this sense, is deferred presence . . . the circulation of signs defers the moment in which we can encounter the thing itself, make it ours, consume or expend it, touch it, see it, intuit its presence . . . this structure presupposes that the sign, which defers presence, is conceivable only on the *basis* of the presence that it defers and *moving toward* the deferred presence that it aims to reappropriate.[16]

As Derrida highlights, signs refer to the absent, a detour that suggests a diversion through language. As a deferral of presence, the sign suggests a 'moving toward' a presence but never an arrival, a supplement or trace that fails to deliver what it promises: 'always differing and deferring, the trace is never as it is in the presentation of itself. It erases itself in presenting itself, muffles itself in resonating.'[17] For the team, language operates as a courier, moving them towards what they imagine is the meaning of the text. Their detour urges them through chains of signifiers that defer arrival, inducing a state of drifting. Just as Navidson and his team struggle to navigate their way through the 'replicating chambers and corridors' (p. 90), their wandering paves the way for further wandering: 'it is almost as if continued use deters the growl and preserves the path they walk' (p. 85). Therefore, their determination to find the transcendental signified of the book results in an even larger space for them to traverse, deferral leads to further deferral and the closer they seem to be to the growl, the further away it sounds. As Derrida suggests, there is 'a certain wandering in the tracing of *différance*',[18] as he demonstrates through his employment of the signifier 'sheaf':

> The word *sheaf* seems to mark more appropriately that the assemblage to be proposed has the complex structure of a weaving, an interlacing which permits the different threads and different lines of meaning – or of force – to go off again in different directions, just as it is always ready to tie itself up with others.[19]

The team's wandering is an aimless drifting to find what cannot be found, producing further lines of association the deeper they read as 'language itself is menaced in its very life, helpless, adrift in the threat of limitlessness'.[20] As a quotation in *House of Leaves*, Seneca writes that 'this is what happens when you hurry through a maze: the faster you go, the worse you are entangled' (p. 115). Navidson's team is caught up in a web of signification, not dissimilar to flies ensnared in a spider's web: the more they struggle to master the web, the more they are tangled within it. For Derrida, 'the figure of the *web* unpacks the appearance of unity presented by a book to reveal an articulation of conflicting messages woven together within it'.[21] With no place of arrival, the team's adventure results in a persistent wandering and 'a sort of nonlocus in which an infinite number of sign-substitutions come into play ... the absence of the transcendental signified extends the domain and the play of signification infinitely'.[22] As a 'particular position, point or place', a locus suggests a specificity of location that the team members so desperately seek. However, through the infinite play of 'sign-substitutions', the team attempts to determine a space that is too large to master.

That the book holds something extremely valuable is indicated through Navidson's initial approach to the book's discovery, when he 'compil[es] a list of possible experts, government agencies, newspapers, periodicals, and television shows they might want to approach' (p. 56). Navidson is so confident that the meaning of the book will be found that he considers the effects of that finding before it has been accomplished. The members of Holloway's team approach the book in the same aggressive manner: 'both Navidson and Holloway

expect to gain a great deal of fame and fortune ... both men agree
their story will guarantee them national attention as well as research
grants and speaking opportunities. Holloway's company will more
than likely thrive' (p. 91). Both men consider how their reading of
the book will result in epic personal gain, as fame, wealth and success
are anticipated. Holloway 'sees what fortune has plopped on his
plate and how famous and rich it could make him, and he wants it.
He wants all of it, immediately, no matter the cost' (p. 82). Like a hunt,
the readers expect their prey to be caught and sold to the highest
bidder. Through their collaborative efforts, they believe their reading
will devour the book, forcing it to be interpreted and ultimately
consumed. As Gavin Young later writes:

> 'Who would have predicted that those two words "discover something"
> would prove the seeds to such unfortunate destruction? The problem,
> of course, was that the certain "something" Holloway so adamantly
> sought to locate never existed per se in that place to begin with.' (p. 95)

On his first reading, Navidson is struck by the size of the space
they are exploring as the endless corridors lead him to a massive
open space whose 'span approaches one mile, making it impossible
to illuminate' (p. 155). He becomes increasingly disorientated in the
space as 'the beam of his flashlight scratches at nothing but the in-
variant blackness' (p. 67). In his attempt to light the darkness, Navidson's
flashlight is unable to force signification in such a large space. In this
way, the space of the book is deceptively large and it seems impossible
that the covers can contain such excess. As Derrida writes in his
essay 'Living on – Border lines', 'the text overruns all the limits
assigned to it so far',[23] and in 'Dissemination',

> writing, fire, erasure, the 'without end', the number, the innumerable,
> are all citations and cited statements about the necessity of these
> citational effects. These effects do not describe the line of a simple
> relation between two texts or two fiery consumptions; they carry you
> off in the displacement of a constellation or a labyrinth. They no
> longer fit 'inside the frame of this piece of paper'. Not only are these
> references infinite, but they conduct you through texts and referral-
> structures that are heterogeneous to each other.[24]

15

The experience of reading conducts the reader toward multiplicity as each signifier requires other signifiers to support its signified. Therefore, the text always signals outside itself, creating a textual web that cannot be contained within its pages, just as the house of *House of Leaves* is larger on the inside than the outside. The 'width of the *house* inside would appear to exceed the width of the *house* as measured from the outside' (p. 30). Such a large space reflects Navidson's experience of the unreadable book where an ultimate signified can never be located. This experience educates Navidson to understand the non-arrival of the book's totality: like the transcendental signified, the prey is endlessly deferred, heard but just out of reach. As 'Plato's pharmacy' explores,

> a text is not a text unless it hides from the first comer, from the first glance, the law of its composition and the rules of its game. A text remains, moreover, forever imperceptible. Its laws and its rules are not, however, harboured in the inaccessibility of a secret; it is simply that they can never be booked, in the *present*, into anything that could rigorously be called a perception.[25]

Like the persistent growl that cannot be located, the text both conceals and reveals. The team that enters the unreadable book is not prepared for the game-playing that reading constitutes. As his final reading indicates, 'maybe the words in the book have been arranged in such a way as to make them practically impossible to read' (p. 467). Such a confusing arrangement of words is clearly aligned with the display of text in *House of Leaves* itself, suggesting echoing dissemination of the signifiers presented.

Because the infinite trajectories of reading induce a sense of disorientation, Navidson is anxious about getting lost in the space of the book. Before the investigatory team begins to read the book, Navidson 'ties one end of some fishing line to the hallway door and then hands the spool to Holloway. "There's almost two miles of line here", he tells him. "Don't let go of it"' (p. 84). To ensure the team does not get lost in the space of the book, Navidson (like Ariadne) has introduced a thread into the maze. Introducing a fishing line into the book further aligns their reading with hunting, a trawling for prey to take the bait, become hooked onto the line and cast into the living room as 'his creep into that place resembles the eerie faith required for any deep sea exploration' (p. 67).

However, the use of the fishing line also positions the team as bait at the end of the hook, bait that will be consumed without ensuring the capture of prey. Because of the depth of their reading, 'Holloway personally takes responsibility for marking their path. He constantly tacks neon arrows to the wall, sprays neon paint on corners, and metes out plenty of fishing line wherever the path becomes especially complicated and twisted' (pp. 118–19). By spraying the walls with neon paint, the team ensure dominance of the space. Holloway instructs 'Jed how to collect scratchings from all the walls they pass along the way' (p. 85). As the team members read the book, they violently scratch the pages in an attempt to capture fragments which can be analysed afterwards. Derrida's essay 'Plato's pharmacy' opens with the definition of the Greek word *Kolaphos*, 'to go into, penetrate . . . to notch, engrave . . . an inscription on a poplar or on the bark of a tree . . . to hollow out, scratch'.[26] Through the associations of these signifiers, the violence of scratching a surface can be aligned with the desire to penetrate. For literary analysts, however, the scratching indicates the necessity to quote from the text, a process that Danielewski deliberately plays with in *House of Leaves*. As an endless tissue of quotations (from both fictional and non-fictional sources) drawn together by Zampanò and a variety of other editorial voices, *House of Leaves* forces the analyst to quote from a quote, deferring its source repetitively. As highlighted earlier, *House of Leaves* presents multiple interpretations of Navidson's attempt to interpret the book that he discovers. Therefore, to quote from this text results in endless quotations of other attempts to interpret. These layers of deferral ensure that the dissemination experienced in the book Navidson reads is also experienced in our reading of *House of Leaves*. However, even quotations from an original source are fraught with anxiety for Derrida: 'let us speak of an "event", nevertheless, and let us use quotation marks to serve as a precaution.'[27] That a precaution might be necessary in order to deal with particular signifiers suggests a simultaneous attempt to curb and admit the infinite play of associations with that particular signifier. These precautionary marks suggest the danger of the sign, the fear of being led into the labyrinth of dissemination. To use quotation marks as a safety measure suggests an attempt to isolate a particular part of the text, and hence limit the disseminative associations of the work as a whole.

The aggression of their reading increases the further they read into the book: 'Holloway succeeds in scratching, stabbing, and ultimately kicking a hole in a wall' (p. 119). As pages of the book, the walls in the hallway are subject to a violent attempt to penetrate, a frustration that originates from the book's 'resistance to representation' (p. 90). Because the pages are 'unreadable', Holloway is determined to force them to signify. As the text is under duress, these attempts begin to consume the book rather than disclose its meaning. Light is positioned as another weapon to assist the team's penetration, 'stabbing into small rooms' (p. 64) in an attempt to force signification. As a subject of enquiry, the book is positioned 'as a patient' (p. 84) as the fictional Leon Robbins suggests: '"Operation" would in fact be a far more appropriate word than "Exploration": Holloway in many ways resembles a conscientious medical practitioner in pre-op' (p. 94). In yet another example of textual play, the text shifts the signifier exploration for operation, aligning the process of reading with a treatment and subsequent curing of the patient. In this way, the book is understood as a subject for examination to be diagnosed, and hence cured, by the reader. Like the monstrosity of illness which posits the unwell subject as different and other to the norm, the unreadable book becomes a subject of horror. The impossibility of reading and interpreting the book is correlated with sickness: the book is not functioning as 'the idea of a totality'.[28] The idea of the book has been traditionally understood as the source of foundational truth for a doctrine or system of thought.[29] Therefore, the book should offer a compact, self-referential read that does not demystify its transcendental signified. As Homi Bhabha writes, 'the discovery of the book installs the sign of appropriate representation: the word of God, truth, art creates the conditions for a beginning, a practice of history and narrative'.[30] However, *House of Leaves* frustrates such a definition, and therefore the book that Navidson cannot decipher requires a cure. In this instance, the prey that is being hunted is the medicine that will result in a readable text. The medicine that the team hope to administer is violent, resulting in a simultaneous cure/poison that can be understood through Derrida's *pharmakon*: 'there is no such thing as a harmless remedy. The *pharmakon* can never be simply beneficial.'[31] In their attempt to force a cure on the text, the team will also destroy it.

In an uncanny echo of the team's initial violence towards the text, the attempt to consume the book results in the gradual consumption of its readers. Their determination to find a cure through any violent means results in their poisoning. Like the *pharmakon*, the cure is also poison. The ability of the book to consume is first indicated through the materials associated with the team of readers: 'Jed begins to notice how more than a few of his buttons have vanished. Strips of Velcro have fallen off his parka, shoe laces have shredded forcing him to bind his boots together with duck tape' (p. 126). The team find 'the remains of one of their foot long neon markers barely clinging to the wall. It has been badly mauled, half of the fabric torn away by some unimaginable claw' (p. 122). The signs enforced on the hallway are consumed, as 'the higher they get, the more the markers have been devoured' (p. 126). 'The house's powerful ability to exorcise any and all things from its midst' (p. 122) suggests the power of the textual both to resist its readers and consume them in turn. As Derrida suggests in 'Plato's pharmacy',

> there is always a surprise in store for the anatomy or physiology of any criticism that might think it had mastered the game, surveyed all the threads at once, deluding itself, too, in wanting to look at the text without touching it, without laying a hand on the 'object', without risking – which is the only chance of entering into the game, by getting a few fingers caught – the addition of some new thread.[32]

As Derrida suggests, the concept of the book as totality is a delusion of mastery and therefore an inadequate reading achieved by keeping the text at a distance. Fearful of 'getting a few fingers caught', the critic must be wary of the power of the text to reinvent itself, refuting signification the more one tries to locate it. Due to multiple textual threads, the team are ensnared within and unprepared for the ability of the book to consume.

Despite the violence of the book towards its readers, Holloway refuses to halt his reading, as 'the prey [is] not killed, the peak [is] not climbed' (p. 124). After the neon markers have been mauled 'a glimmer of joy flickers across Holloway's features, as if finally

something about that place has begun to make sense' (p. 123).Through
the endless repetition of the signifiers, the text induces madness in
Holloway who is convinced the growl is a presence:

> For Holloway, it is impossible to merely accept the growl as a quality of
> that place anymore. Upon seeing the torn marker and their lost water,
> he seems to transfigure the eerie sound into an utterance made by some
> definitive creature, thus providing him with something concrete to pursue.
> Holloway almost seems drunk as he rushes after the sound. (pp. 123–4)

Holloway has been enticed by the growl, which has acted like bait
to lead him deeper into insanity as he eventually shoots both his team
members and himself. 'Wax is back for a second chug [of water],
when the crack of a rifle drops him to the floor, blood immediately
gushing from his left armpit' (p. 126). As 'Dr Haugeland'[33] suggests,
'"knowledge is hot water on wool. It shrinks time and space . . .
boredom, due to repetition *stretches* time and space"' (p. 167). The
endless repetition consumes Holloway as his boredom has the ability
to enlarge the space further. As 'Dr Helen Hodge'[34] suggests, '"in
those endlessly repetitive hallway and stairs, there is nothing for us
to connect with. That permanently foreign place does not excite
us. It bores us"' (p. 167).

This boredom is evident as the book that Navidson and his team
are reading does not entertain, it is not a totality. Instead, the book
leads the reader down several pathways with no clear definable meaning. As Derrida suggests, 'in the delineation of *différance* everything
is strategic and adventurous . . . adventurous because this strategy is
not a simple strategy in the sense that strategy orients tactics according to a final goal'.[35] Instead of an eventual arrival, the text celebrates
the explosive adventure of the attempt to arrive there. After he has
committed suicide, 'fingers of blackness slash across the lighted wall
and consume Holloway' (p. 338) as 'the creature Holloway hunts
has already begun to feed on him' (p. 334). Because Navidson has
attempted to consume the book, he is also consumed by it. After
the final exploration, he is rushed to hospital and survives, although
'frostbite claimed his right hand and clipped the top portion of one
ear. Patches of skin on his face were also removed as well as his left
eye' (p. 523). Furthermore, his hip had 'inexplicably shattered and

had to be replaced. Doctors said he would need a crutch for the rest of his life' (p. 523). Therefore, Navidson's reading quest has detrimental effects on his health as the violence he brings to the book is inflicted upon him in turn. Significantly, the loss of his left eye affects his ability to read and serves as a warning for others who attempt such a violent reading.

In his frustration with the book, Navidson states: '"Actually, I'd like to burn it down. Can't think clearly enough to do it though"' (p. 5). This is reiterated in his letter to Karen, 'I should burn the place down, forget about it' (p. 389). These repeated references to burning suggest the ultimate consumption. As a final attempt to read the unreadable text, Navidson 'turns his attention to the last possible activity, the only book in his possession: *House of Leaves*' (p. 465). It is only when the book is about to be destroyed that it is revealed: throughout *House of Leaves*, Navidson and his team have been reading *House of Leaves*. Danielewski's text presents multiple interpretations (from fictional and non-fictional points of reference) of Navidson's attempt to interpret those very interpretations. Therefore, Navidson is both reader and subject of the book he attempts to interpret. This web of uncertainty is the disseminative maze that readers have been experiencing throughout. Therefore, the book Navidson is exploring is both inside and outside of Danielewski's text, functioning both as a quotation within it and a gesturing outside it. Deconstruction has been defined as 'the careful teasing out of warring forces of signification *within the text itself*'.[36] These forces portray the paradox of Navidson's position. As both reader and subject, Navidson experiences an uncanny doubling as he reads about himself reading. Paradoxically, he is both inside (as subject) and outside (as reader) the book, located in an impossible contradictory space that can only result in his consumption as he effectively cancels himself out. It is only when Navidson refers to the book as an object that we begin to understand his dangerous position within it. Like someone who watches his own actions as he is performing them, Navidson repeatedly attempts to reread himself, producing an even larger maze of interpretations in which to wander, lost. Through his paradoxical position he is swallowed up by the enormity of the book.

After being lost for so long, the 'last possible activity' available to Navidson is to destroy the book. By referring to the book as an object, Navidson attempts to quote the book, situating himself outside it. This is, however, impossible as *House of Leaves* charts him reading *House of Leaves*, and the destruction of the book is therefore still within the book. By attempting to refute a paradoxical inside, Navidson desires to situate the book as nothing more than pages that can be mastered through destruction. Hence, the violence of his reading culminates in a final consumption that will attempt to erase the horror of the unreadable text, a burning that he has already read himself attempt. In relation to *House of Leaves*, Catherine Spooner suggests that 'the book/house is a self-consuming artefact'.[37] While offering itself to the violence of reading, the book consumes itself as demonstrated by Navidson's contradictory position within it. His objectification of the book permits both his and its self-consumption. As he consumes the book he will also read it: 'he tears out the first page, which of course consists of two pages of text, and rolls it into a tight stick, thus creating a torch which will burn for about two minutes and provide him with just enough time to read the next two pages' (p. 467). This final act of consumption highlights the violence of reading, as the desire to read is simultaneously the desire to consume.

As Derrida explores in *The Post Card*, 'above all language remains self-evidently secret, as if it were being invented at every step, and as if it were burning immediately, as soon as any third party would set eyes on it'.[38] The cryptic nature of the text results in a desire to unweave it through a violence that burns the text as it is read. Reading, therefore, is burning: 'and as the fire rapidly devours the paper, Navidson's eyes frantically sweep down over the text, keeping just ahead of the necessary immolation' (p. 467). Each word is consumed immediately after it is read, as if Navidson's eyes rather than the fire were burning the page. As an immolation, the burning of the book functions as a sacrifice for Navidson to maintain mastery over it. As Malabou writes, 'for Derrida, legibility is death. To give something to be read is to rush headlong towards death, to kill, to consign to the flames.'[39] For Derrida, to read is to attempt to master and therefore, reading is bound with violence. As he writes in 'Outwork', 'the book form alone can no longer settle – here for example – the case of those writing processes which, in *practically* questioning that form, must also dismantle it'.[40]

To continue reading, Navidson is forced to 'light the cover of the book as well as the spine' (p. 467) as the light emitted does not give him time to read the whole text again. 'He tries to read faster, inevitably loses some of the text, frequently burns his fingers. In the end Navidson is left with one page and one match. For a long time he waits in darkness and cold, postponing this final bit of illumination.' (p. 467) His violation of the text extends further as he 'loses' parts of the text. As Derrida highlighted earlier, 'any criticism that might think it had mastered the game, surveyed all the threads at once, is deluding itself, too, in wanting to look at the text without touching it'.[41] Navidson's final reading results in an inaccurate, delusional one that resists the text in its disseminative entirety. However, he is not unscathed by his own violence, as his fingers are burnt by his reading:

> At last though, he grips the match by the neck and after locating the friction strip sparks to life a final ball of light. First, he reads a few lines by match light and then as the heat bites his fingertips he applies the flame to the page. Here then is one end: a final act of reading, a final act of consumption. (p. 467)

In burning the object, Navidson attempts to reaffirm the totality of the book as 'a great complexity intrudes, tearing apart, piece by piece, all of [his] carefully conceived denials' (p. xxiii). As Homi Bhabha suggests, 'the institution of the word in the wilds is also an *Enstellung*, a process of displacement, distortion, dislocation, repetition – the dazzling light of literature sheds only areas of darkness'.[42] After the realization that there is no transcendental signified, Navidson attempts to destroy the source of his frustrations, and therefore, in destruction, determine the text.

Navidson's last interaction with the text results in a page aflame as the totality of the book disintegrates: 'as he reaches the last few words, flames lick around his hands, ash peels off into the surrounding emptiness, and then as the fire retreats, dimming, its light suddenly spent, the book is gone leaving nothing behind but invisible traces already dismantled in the dark' (p. 467). Although the object of the book has been destroyed, traces remain, scattered into tiny cinders of itself as 'the book is burning [and therefore is] shattered into specters of dust' (p. 518). In this way, the burning of the book only produces further dissemination:

> consumption is, like dissemination, textual through and through. Which does not mean that it is reduced (to ashes) but that your thinking about the text has been set on fire. The fact that, cut off from any ultimate, 'real' referent – which would keep the fire at a reassuring distance – this sort of consumption seems to consume only traces, ashes, and to shed light on nothing that would be present, in no way prevents it from burning.[43]

Although the book has been burnt, the network of associations that have plagued Navidson remain in his mind. Therefore, it is his mind which has been ignited (hence his burning injuries) as his reading became so violent that his 'thinking about the text has been set on fire'. Instead of the triumph he anticipated from removing the book as object, he is left with a burning within, just as instead of being within the book, the book has become within him. Through the power of the text, the boundary between book and reader is challenged.

The game that is *House of Leaves* manipulates the reader into becoming both reader and subject, and just as the reader enters the text, she must permit the book entry to herself.[44] As a book of repeated interpretations of Navidson's attempt to interpret those interpretations, *House of Leaves* is only too aware of the disorder of reading, a process that celebrates multiplicity and undecidability. As explored in 'Plato's pharmacy', with 'textuality being constituted by differences and by differences from differences, it is by nature absolutely heterogeneous and is constantly composing with the forces that tend to annihilate it'.[45] This is why 'it is difficult to analyse the book without merely repeating what is already within it'.[46] Although the haunted text in *House of Leaves* is also the hunted text, the ability of the book to wound cannot be in doubt.

2

The Horror of Miscommunication:
The Story of Lucy Gault

ൔ

This chapter will explore the catastrophic results of miscommunication. In *The Story of Lucy Gault* a misleading event triggers a chain
reaction of misinterpretation which leads to a horror that cannot
be spoken, an unnecessary fear that fuels a silence of loss. In Trevor's
text, misinterpretation of the written word is considered alongside
the misreading of certain events through misleading signs. Through
the misreading of a particular event, the child protagonist, Lucy, is
assumed dead; the horror that cannot be spoken is the fear that she
has taken her own life. Because of the misleading event, an attempt
to communicate (both orally and through writing) results in further
miscommunication. After the inaccurate assumption, her parents
embark on a journey of mourning initiated by her counterfeit suicide.
Their pathway is understood as a wandering without arrival[1] as
determined by letters that do not arrive or are not sent. After thirty
years, Lucy's father returns home to the realization that his daughter
was found alive in the woods shortly after his departure, and so his
journey of wandering was unnecessary as was his wife's guilt-induced
premature death. Such a catastrophe is initiated by misinterpretation,
the horror of the unspeakable and the failure of a letter to reach its
destination.

William Trevor's text *The Story of Lucy Gault* suggests a haunted
pathway of lost communication when letters do not arrive at their
destination and oral attempts to communicate are misinterpreted

or not attempted. Trevor's text is in dialogue with Derrida's *The Post Card*[2] and Catherine Malabou's text *Counterpath: Traveling with Jacques Derrida*.[3] As Derrida proposes, all letters are postcards open to multiple others on a journey fraught with imprecision. As the term 'destinerrance' suggests, the 'being-destined-to-wander of the message and of destining itself' results in 'sending as a gamble'.[4] Therefore, letters are always 'in the process of arriving'.[5] Through the interaction of these three texts, this chapter will suggest that the fraught pathway of letter-sending can be aligned with a fractured lineage, an alternative pathway that spans the multiple directions of misinterpretation.[6] Letters are revealed to be simultaneously cryptic and open, lacking the privacy reassured by the postal service and coded through the dissemination of meaning associated with all signifiers. As Derrida writes: '"deconstruction" would, in a word, be a certain experience of the voyage, of letters and of language *en voyage*.'[7]

The narrative pathway of *The Story of Lucy Gault* is initiated by the misinterpretation of an item of clothing found in close proximity to the sea. After being told she and her parents are moving away from her beloved home Lahardane, eight-year-old Lucy runs away. As Catherine Malabou explores in relation to the suffix 'strophe', a catastrophe involves a 'turning toward in the sense of swirling, failing to remain still, or wandering'.[8] Therefore, Lucy's wandering initiates catastrophe in her parents' lives, a journey that results in a disjointed pathway of mourning. As her father, Everard, searches for her, he finds Lucy's vest caught amongst the stones of the coastline and assumes she has taken her own life in the sea. The sign of her vest therefore indicates a falsehood as 'time made truth of what appeared to be. The days that passed, in becoming weeks, still did not disturb the surface an assumption had created . . . the single sandal found among the rocks became a sodden image of death.'[9] This assumption produces a skewed pathway that results in a time out of joint.[10] Such a misinterpretation is reinforced by the housekeeper, Bridget, and her suspicions that Lucy used to swim alone in secret. '"I'm not saying she ever said a word, ma'am. It's only Henry and myself thought it. We should have said it to you, sir."'[11] Bridget's revelation of the secret is itself secretive as their knowledge is only conjecture. That Lucy could keep such a secret from her parents suggests a lack of communication throughout the Gault household. Through the misreading of the vest, the lives of the family are permanently altered: 'chance, not wrath, had this summer ordered the fate of the Gaults' (p. 36). The power of miscommunication is evident through a perceived death that is not a death at all. Although alive, Lucy is killed through misinterpretation, and is condemned to the status of living dead.

Such a detrimental misunderstanding is foregrounded by multiple instances of miscommunication, particularly between Lucy and her parents, Heloise and Everard. Discussing their imminent departure, Lucy highlights how 'everything she said to them on the way back they didn't hear. They didn't want to hear, they didn't want to listen' (p. 17). In her frustration, Lucy's only method of communication is to run away. However, this attempt is misinterpreted and her communication is never achieved. After her disappearance, Everard realizes that their reasons for leaving Ireland were not adequately explained to their daughter.

> 'We told her lies,' the Captain said before they reached the place. Heloise didn't understand. Then she remembered the reassurances and the half promises, and remembered knowing that the promises might not be kept. Disobedience had been a child's defiance, deception the coinage they had offered her themselves. (p. 31)

Lucy's disappearance and misread death occurs because the Gaults did not communicate effectively with their daughter: 'to their child she had not explained enough' (p. 34). Their fabrications incur a sense of distrust which fractures their relationship. As Lucy is aware, 'all the time they were pretending' (p. 17). In addition to permanently altering her childhood, such falsehoods continue to determine Lucy throughout her life. Lucy's correct interpretation of her parents' lies determines her subsequent course of action: she inherits their inability to communicate effectively as she tries to demonstrate her fears of leaving by running away. Ironically, running away from her beloved home is an attempt to reveal her refusal to leave that very home. In order to soothe her fears of leaving Lahardane, Everard and Heloise's false reassurances effectively kill their child: 'that a child's anxieties had been impatiently ignored was the cruelty that remained' (p. 156). The narratives supposed to reassure their daughter have devastating consequences. As Bridget's husband, Henry, notices: 'she hadn't spoken a word to him for three days, nor to Bridget either' (p. 28). However, Lucy's silence is noted but not interpreted. As she realizes she is not able to communicate with her parents, she discusses with her father how

> the first time he was in Enniseala, he said, was when he was five, brought in to have the fraenulum of his tongue cut.
> 'What's fraenulum?'
> 'A little snag underneath your tongue. If it's too tight you're tongue-tied.'
> 'What's tongue-tied?'
> 'It's when you can't speak clearly.'
> 'And couldn't you?'
> 'They said I couldn't.' (pp. 14–15)

Through their inability to communicate, Lucy reminds her father of his own inability to communicate effectively as a child. As such, she requires a definition of 'tongue-tied', determining how, with a short fraenulum, the tongue is restricted in its ability to produce speech. As her father highlights, the ability to communicate effectively is determined by others as 'they' determined he could not speak properly. Her father's definition by others mirrors Lucy's subsequent construction as an outcast in the society where she lives. Similarly, Lucy encourages her father to discuss a mute fisherman:

> 'There's a fisherman in Kilauran can't speak at all,' she said.
> 'I know.'
> 'He does it on his fingers.'
> 'Yes, he does.'
> 'You see him doing it. The other fishermen understand him.' (p. 15)

Although only a child, Lucy highlights her inability to communicate effectively with her father through reference to a man without speech. Although mute, the fisherman can communicate clearly, allowing Lucy to highlight that there are more effective methods of communication than speech.

After Lucy's supposed death, the convoluted pathway of mourning that her parents undergo is shadowed by multiple instances of failed communication. After Lucy is found, she 'was starved, so weak you'd say she couldn't live: unspoken, these comments tumbled about in Bridget's thoughts' (p. 41). As soon as he hears the news, the family lawyer, Sullivan, attempts to contact her parents via telegram, '*Lucy found alive in the woods,* the message had gone to England' (p. 45). Cast into the role of orphan, Lucy is taken in by Bridget and Henry, servants and family friends of the Gaults. As representative of the law, Sullivan fails in his attempt to inform his clients that their daughter is indeed alive. In doing so, he 'kept the depth of his concern private' (p. 69). Although the telegram arrives at its destination, the message is not received by its destined recipients. After changing their plans, the Gaults have moved on from the address they left behind. Therefore, a fundamental flaw of the postal system is revealed, as the receiving of letters depends on the permanence of the addressee. Because the Gaults are in transit, they do not receive the vital information that could save their lives and halt their journey of mourning. In this way, the wandering parents are never permanently located, and therefore remain uncontactable. In contrast, Lucy is left lame after her disobedient wandering and remains chained to Ireland; she is a locatable recipient and yet does not hear from her parents. To successfully send and receive, addressee and addresser depend upon an impossible permanence. As a servant in the household asks, 'would we send another wire, sir, in case that one would have gone astray?' (p. 49). Such anxiety highlights the potential for every sending not to arrive at its destination. Like the attempt to communicate verbally, there are multiple routes open to letters that are alternative to the destined path. As Derrida writes in *The Post Card,* 'the letter is immediately dispersed or multiplied, a divided echo of itself . . . it is lost for the addressee at the very second when it is inscribed, its destination is immediately multiple, anonymous'.[12] As 'the site of all transferences and all correspondences',[13] the postal service is 'an anonymous third party, a neutral machinery that supposedly leads the message to its destination'.[14] As a third party, the postal service acts as an interceptor, a courier that reduces the chance of a letter's arrival as 'an intercepted letter . . . is without value'.[15] Because of the Gaults' constant movement, the vital information is never received, their wandering lasts for thirty years and results in the death of Lucy's mother, Heloise.

The failure to contact Lucy's parents is also due to the unspeakable nature of their child's supposed suicide.[16] In fear of finding her child's body on the shore, Heloise admits that 'there is, for me, a horror I do not want to know' (p. 34). As an event that assumes a child's decision to die, Lucy's suicide is a horror that exceeds traditional understandings of the child: '"it couldn't be that," Bridget whispered' (p. 30). Instead of openly stating the event they all fear has happened, witnesses utilize language in such a way as to circumvent the subject: even the servants do not utter that which cannot be spoken. As a grieving mother, Heloise insists on silencing the subject, framing it as a forbidden topic with her husband, and therefore neither can discuss their daughter's death. Hence the miscommunication that resulted in a destructive misreading leads to further silences between husband and wife or 'artificial conversation' (p. 83). After Lucy's 'death', communication between Heloise and Everard Gault completely breaks down: 'one spoke, the other hardly heard' (p. 35). As Heloise admits to herself but not to her husband, 'a rented villa in a Sussex suburb was not far enough away: for days she'd known that, but had not said it' (p. 36). As the couple travel away from the site of horror, their ability to communicate with one another becomes more and more impaired: 'in fits and starts the conversation would drift about – never to Lahardane or to Ireland' (p. 57). Through her unnecessary mourning, Heloise imposes a censorship on her lost daughter as 'another child, so long denied them, might one day be born in Italy ... but they were wary of expectation, drew back from it as they did from what must not be spoken of. Expert now at altering sentences already begun, or allowing them to wither ...' (p. 57). For her parents, the subject of Lucy occupies the cryptic and the secretive, and therefore cannot be uttered. By exceeding the boundaries of language, Lucy is without signification and therefore both under-signified by her family and over-signified by strangers as her story becomes a legend. As the couple near this particular topic of conversation, the horror of such an event imposes strict barriers ensuring the subject cannot be approached. As Heloise demonstrates, pathways of conversation must be diverted away from a route that cannot be taken.

She hadn't been able to explain why it was that she would always want to forget. But in the morning she would do better. She heard

---

her voice apologising and talking then of all she didn't want to talk
about; before she closed her eyes she found the sentences came quite
easily. But when she slept, and woke after a few minutes, she heard
herself saying she couldn't have that conversation and knew that she
was right. (p. 84)

In a double censoring, Heloise cannot communicate her need to
avoid the subject of her daughter's 'death'. Although she envisions
an attempt to communicate, the reality of daybreak quickly convinces
her otherwise. Just as Lucy has become a horror story that cannot
be spoken, Heloise produces a narrative of herself as 'she heard her
voice apologising' and 'heard herself saying she couldn't have that
conversation' (p. 84). Through the construction of a dual self, Heloise
highlights the failure of fabrications: although she imagines it, her
'other' self cannot induce communication. Therefore, although she
becomes aware of the futility of constructions, she cannot apply this
to Lucy.

After their departure, Everard's attempt to contact Ireland fails
due to his wife's imposed censorship:

He had written to Ireland . . . more than once he had written, but
each time had drawn back when the moment of posting came. There
would be a reply, surreptitiously received, a secret correspondence
begun, the breaking of the trust that had always been there in his
marriage. He kept the letters hidden, their envelopes stamped. (p. 83)

Out of loyalty to his wife, 'not wanting ever to know the news from
Ireland' (p. 174), Everard halts at the moment of posting as 'a letter
would bring a reply that would have to be suppressed' (p. 144). Because
Heloise censors the horror of their child's 'death', she and Everard do
not contact Ireland to learn that the horror was entirely their own
construction. Like their initial misinterpretation, Heloise's imposed
censorship kills her daughter. In this way, Lucy becomes a fabrication
to her parents just as she becomes a legend to society. Like letters
written in wartime, where 'parts of the few letters were blackly
smudged out, or so cut away by the army censors that both sides of
a page were deprived' (p. 130), Lucy becomes an incomplete narrative,
her identity both censored and sensationalized. Just as information

in wartime can be dangerous, the circumstances of her death become hazardous to her parents' health, and therefore also have to be 'smudged out'.

Although they remain unposted, Everard's letters retain the stamp of their entry into the postal system. After returning to his daughter, he 'told [her] how he had stamped each envelope, how he had afterwards kept the letters by him' (p. 174). Although the censorship that binds him to his wife means that they cannot be posted, Everard keeps the letters as reaffirmation of the unspeakable horror of his daughter. By writing letters that he does not send, her father reaffirms her death as too horrific to speak of, as censorship is reinforced through writing. As Malabou writes, 'legibility is death. To give something to be read is to rush headlong towards death, to kill, to consign to the flames';[17] therefore, writing has the ability to censure rather than signify. As Derrida suggests in relation to the letter being simultaneously open and closed (and therefore a postcard), 'when I write, right here, on these innumerable post cards, I annihilate not only what I am saying but also the unique addressee that I constitute, and therefore every possible addressee, and every destination'.[18] Therefore, Everard's construction of Lucy through text (just as she is constructed through silence) results in further miscommunication as Lucy is killed both by misinterpretation of her 'death' and the subsequent inaccurate narratives that determine her. As Everard tells Lucy, 'years later he had dropped them, one by one, into the fire and watched the blackened paper curling before it fell away' (p. 174). Burning the letters suggests the horror of a topic that must be censored, reinforcing the strict censorship imposed by his wife.

Just as she has become a horror in her parents' minds, Lucy becomes monstrous to those around her and also to herself. When she is found in the woods by Henry, her 'lips were stained with blackberry juice. There was a sick look about her, her cheeks fallen in, dark hollows beneath her eyes, her hair as ragged as a tinker's' (p. 40). Aesthetically, Lucy has become the monstrosity that her parents cannot bear to talk about. As her attempt to run away was thwarted by a broken ankle, her 'whole leg had gone useless, trailing like something dead . . . the child was dirty all over, her feet, her hands, her hair tangled, scratches on her arms and face. Her ribs stood out, the flesh of her stomach loose beneath them' (p. 43). Uncannily, Lucy's body exhibits the construction she has become not only in her parents' minds but also in society. As Bridget suggests, 'she'd never seen the likes of the poor creature when Henry brought her in, death's door you'd have said' (p. 49). What cannot be spoken about manifests itself in her appearance, as that which is hidden and concealed uncannily comes to light.[19] Both familiar and unfamiliar, Lucy is both herself and some other being, an uncanny distortion of who she once was. As Bridget outlines, 'she had blood oozing out from the scratches on her face. She could taste it and it frightened her' (p. 47). As explored in other Gothic texts, horror is aligned with what cannot conventionally be signified or understood. As Botting writes, 'horror marks the response to an excess that cannot be transcended'.[20] Like the living dead, Lucy has the appearance of the barely alive. With her skin stained with blood and blackberry juice, 'hollows beneath her eyes', 'hair ragged' and her leg being dragged behind her, Lucy clearly occupies the realm of the Gothic monster. As Clive Bloom suggests: 'the body, its fluids, passages and surfaces, is the registration for horror's symbolic significance'.[21] As a Gothic child, her youth further exaggerates her horrific aesthetic position. Because of her sensational history and subsequent isolation, Lucy is a horror to be shied away from.

Although her appearance improves with care and nourishment, Lucy has a limp for the rest of her life, ensuring she is an outcast in the small village she inhabits: 'Mrs McBride would try not to stare at her. Everyone tried not to. Mr Aylward had stared at first. Just once she saw him. They stared at her for what she'd done; they stared at her limp' (p. 63). Stained by her disobedience, Lucy's limp becomes an indicator of the horror that has constructed her life, forcing her into a liminal role that casts her as a monstrous figure. Even Ralph, the man she loves, admits that 'her limp made her more herself' (p. 101), as if her difference were the determining aspect of her identity. As she observes at school, 'in the play-yard Edie Hosford still didn't want to come near to her' (p. 63). As Bloom writes, 'the fear of the horror object is "usually" associated with fear of *contact* (here interpreted as fear of *pollution*) . . . felt through the reactions of the physical body'.[22] After the event that has marked her for life, others become fearful of contact with Lucy Gault, as if her monstrosity might contaminate them. Deformed and outcast by her guilt, Lucy is aligned with the unnatural and the illegal. As

Botting suggests, 'horror describes the movement of contraction and recoil'.[23]

Although she is unable to communicate about the event that has determined her, she herself becomes a legendary talking point:

> While at Lahardane there was the rawness of disorder, the story of what had brought it so dramatically to a country house came to find a place among the stories that were told in the neighbourhood . . . the tragedy called down upon herself by a child, and what had since become her life, made a talking point and seemed to strangers to be the material of legend . . . conversation in back bars, at tea tables and card tables, was enlivened by reports of what had occurred. (pp. 69–70)

In contrast with the censorship of her family, Lucy is the source of immense communication in society. However, 'as often with such travellers' tales, exaggeration improved the telling. Borrowed facts, sewn in where there was a dearth, gathered authority with repetition' (p. 70). Lucy becomes a construction in the eyes of others, a warning of the dangers of misbehaviour that reduce an individual to a monster. As Roland Barthes suggests about myth: 'every object in the world can pass from a closed, silent existence to an oral state, open to appropriation by society, for there is no law, whether natural or not, which forbids talking about things.'[24] As a figure of curiosity and difference, Lucy is positioned as a subject for scrutiny and discussion, reinforcing her self-perception as monstrous. After Sullivan's visit Lucy tells Henry that '"he doesn't like me"' (p. 55). Her response to the lawyer clearly indicates that she aligns herself with the illegal. Similarly, a visit to a local shop incurs the following response from Lucy: 'Mrs McBride didn't like her any more even though she'd given her the biscuit. Mrs McBride was the same as everyone else' (p. 64). Even as she approaches her forties, Lucy is aware of her construction by others, as 'often she wondered if she caused a nervousness in the people of Enniseala, since strange events must have left her strange' (p. 196). Events of an extraordinary nature determine her as other throughout her life.

In addition to her injuries, Lucy remains in 'mute denial' (p. 53) after she is found, 'so silent now she might never open her mouth again' (p. 42). As her parents cannot bear to talk about her, she becomes unable to communicate herself, silenced as a subject by her over-determination by others. Her position as a monstrous curiosity grows as she ages and reconsiders her disastrous decision to run away: '"Was I possessed?"' (p. 118). Because of her guilt, Lucy is susceptible to the narrative of herself and believes she is aligned with the demonic. As Sullivan suggests to Bridget: 'my mother used to say you could find the Devil in a child' (p. 48). In further consideration of her status as legend, Lucy aligns herself with a fictional character from *Jane Eyre*: '"Like poor Mrs Rochester! Whom nobody had sympathy for!"' (p. 118). Like Mrs Rochester, Lucy is determined as a villainous construction, a 'madwoman in the attic'.[25] Hidden away and referred to as a spectral presence, Rochester's first wife is hideous in appearance and actions: 'at the further end of the room, a figure ran backwards and forwards. What it was, whether beast or human being, one could not, at first sight, tell.'[26] Just as she is determined by others as a narrative construction, Lucy begins to comprehend herself through likenesses to fictional characters. Like an inherited stigma, Lucy insists that '"I have to live with it until they return"' (p. 119). As an 'it' her guilt becomes embodied. Just as her parents' return signifies an end to their journey of mourning, Lucy hopes their arrival will dissolve the horror that has determined her identity. Although Lucy believes she was possessed by love for her home, it is only after the event that she becomes possessed by the multitude of voices that shape her fragmented sense of identity. As her father observes, 'his daughter's brooding years had created something of their own that long ago had possessed her, wrapping her like fog that chilled' (p. 156). Like 'fog that chilled', Lucy is separated from others by barriers that are both self-imposed and created by external forces in reaction to horror.

Lucy's inability to communicate extends to the man she loves, Ralph. As his employer explains to him, '"I imagine you weren't told what happened at Lahardane"' (p. 87). During their first (accidental) meeting, Ralph realizes that 'the girl who'd come out of the house hadn't said her name' (p. 86). Ashamed of the associations aligned with her, Lucy initially attempts to conceal her past from Ralph, and he therefore learns of her narrative from others. 'Ralph listened while the Ryalls told the story between them, Mr Ryall factual and precise, his wife supplying emotional overtones' (pp. 87–8). As their relationship develops, it becomes fraught with miscommunication: 'he wanted to ask her about that time but could not' (p. 109) The single event that has defined Lucy is barred from discussion even with the man she loves. 'One day in the woods she suddenly said, "We must go back", as if she sensed his longing to hear what she might have said, as if she feared it' (p. 109). Like her parents, Lucy desperately seeks alternative pathways of communication to avoid the unspeakable event. In an uncanny replication, Lucy and Ralph become like Everard and Heloise, unable to speak to one another. 'When Ralph began to answer he felt that what he said was hardly heard' (p. 119). As Derrida explores in *The Post Card*, love becomes subject to forces of miscommunication: '"How can we forget today?" she whispered and was not heard. "I could never not love you", Ralph said, and this was lost as well' (p. 117). Although she loves Ralph, she denies herself the happiness of marriage, insisting that '"I'm not someone to love"' (p. 111). As she has been constructed a monster, Lucy believes she does not deserve Ralph's love as 'the nature and the tenets of her life had already been laid down for her' (p. 81). Furthermore, because the foundations of their relationship are based on the construction that is Lucy Gault, their relationship is doomed to failure. In his first encounter with Ralph, clergyman Canon Crosbie asserts that '"I'm told you've been to Lahardane"' and that '"You met Lucy Gault, I heard"' (p. 92). Immediately, Lucy's relationship with Ralph is public knowledge, an additional chapter to the legend of her existence. As Ralph notes, 'there was an implication in what was being said' (p. 92), suggesting that their relationship is determined by those that surround them. Such involvement causes embarrassment for Ralph, who 'would have liked to bring the encounter to an end, but didn't quite know how to do so' (p. 93). Encouraged to 'give a little company to a young girl who lacks the company of her own generation', Canon Crosbie's 'wordy hyperbole' (p. 94) ensures that, even in love, Lucy continues to be determined by others. Although Ralph denies his prior knowledge to Lucy, he admits that 'far from adversely affecting his attachment, the story that was renowned in Enniseala strengthened it' (p. 99). In spite of his feelings for her, Ralph's attraction depends upon the manufactured fabrications he has heard: '*Lucy Gault*, he saw written down, as she had written it. No other name could be as right' (p. 101). Like other members of society, his love is contaminated by a sense of curiosity to gaze upon the legend that is Lucy Gault. Instead of Lucy being the source of contamination, she is polluted by the fears of others.

After his wife's death, Everard returns to Ireland to realize that his daughter is still alive. However, after such a time, their relationship is irreparable as the failure of communication and the letter results in a dislocated family. As the narrative suggests, 'what fluke . . . what perversity had been at play' (p. 54) to induce such a dislocated set of events. Due to the misreading of an event, the lineage of the Gaults is halted as 'their people would end when they did' (p. 165): there is no heir to inherit their estate. Through her disobedience, Lucy refuses herself marriage and children with the man she loves, as she has condemned herself to wait for her parents' return in order to seek redemption. As she explains to Ralph, '"I long for their forgiveness. That will not just go away"' (p. 118). Just as her parents have contributed to her construction as a monstrosity, she must wait for their arrival in order to escape this fabrication. In addition to their forgiveness, Lucy wants to repair the gulf of miscommunication between her and her parents: '"what do they think, Ralph, and do not say? Why do they not come back?"' (p. 119). As the act of running away was an attempt to communicate with her parents, Lucy is never able to translate this initial silence to them: a minor miscommunication leads to major misinterpretations that are never resolved. The assumption that her parents have constructed the event of her 'death' haunts her as she desires to correct it: '"I did not hate them, yet how do they know it, any more than they know all they so easily might?"' (p. 119). As she has been determined a horror by the society that surrounds her, Lucy is aware that her parents may have a similar misapprehension regarding her 'death'. Her lengthy wait for their return is fuelled by a determination to clear her name. Like a wronged criminal, Lucy desperately wants to correct the misreading of her actions as a child. Before the event that changes their lives, Lucy describes how her father 'wrote with a pebble on the sand. *Lucy Gault*, he wrote. "Now, that's a lovely name"' (p. 22). Before such a detrimental misinterpretation, her father insists on the loveliness of her name. However, after the event that constructs Lucy Gault as a horror, the signification of her name changes irreversibly. As a disgraced orphan, her name becomes aligned with the multitude of stories told by the society that surrounds her. Hence her name becomes a fragmented fabrication of assumption, a construction she desperately wants to change. However, the assumptions built by miscommunication are so strong that, after thirty years, she cannot challenge them. As her mother died without knowing the truth, Lucy's guilt is exaggerated as she becomes her mother's murderer. As her father informs her: "'I can't not tell you that the guilt your mother felt was a bit too much for her'" (p. 175).

Ultimately, Lucy's determination as monstrous cannot be undone as the most powerful constructions are built through miscommunication. As her father admits, 'he tried to imagine her at fourteen, at seventeen, at twenty; but his memory of her as an infant in his arms, or when he had been concerned about her as a child too much on her own, more potently intervened' (p. 165). Instead of negotiating Lucy's existence as an adult, Everard cannot move away from his construction of her as a child. 'His instinct when in his daughter's company was to reach out for her hand, seeking the child she'd been, as if in touching her he would somehow find what had been lost to him. But the instinct was each time stifled' (p. 155). Although he reassures her through words, his actions signify a very different position as he cannot bear to touch her, reinforcing her position as a monster. Due to the cruelty of the situation, Everard cannot forgive his daughter for an event that has dislocated their family. For her parents and indeed society as a whole, Lucy did die as a child, and therefore her position as an adult is akin to that of the living dead: 'she should have died a child; she knows that but has never said it' (p. 227). Although a living adult, Lucy is forever aligned with a dead child.

After her father returns, Lucy realizes the futility of her decision to wait for a communication that is impossible. 'What terrible folly had possessed her? All these years to have so stubbornly waited for no more than an old man's shattered words?' (p. 170). Like all other communication in the text, his words fail to provide what she desperately seeks. As his words are 'shattered', the only terms her father can offer are fragmented, horrified by the autonomy of a situation that is entirely out of his control. His initial sighting of his daughter reinforces her position as spectral as 'he saw his daughter in the pasture fields and in a moment of confusion thought she was his wife' (p. 153). The moment of their reunion lacks sentiment and emotion, indicative of the wider breakdown in communication that ordered their fate.

> 'Who are you?' she asked, her voice her mother's also.
> . . . 'Don't you know me?'
> 'No.'
> 'Look at me, Lucy,' the Captain said, reaching the bottom of the stairs.
> 'What do you want? Why should I know you?'
> They gazed at one another. Her cheeks had gone as white as the dress she wore and he knew that she recognised him then. She did not say anything and he stood still, not going closer to her. (p. 153)

Instead of a dramatic meeting, father and daughter are caught in a web of silence. As a topic that has been censored for so long, Everard remains distanced from Lucy whose guilt cannot be overturned. 'In spite of all he said in terms of contrition and regret, the Captain was aware he could not say enough' (p. 156). As his attempt to communicate fails, he realizes he cannot deliver Lucy from her status as an outcast. 'It concerned him that she never went in to Enniseala, that as an adult she had never walked in its long main street' (p. 165). As occurred after the event of Lucy's 'death', attempts to communicate often result in further miscommunication. As he admits, 'conversation was still easier with Bridget or with Henry than with his own daughter' (p. 164). The suspected horror that his daughter has represented for so long remains with him as 'the two sat at either end of the long table in the dining-room, which was where their conversations mostly occurred, although as often as not nothing at all was said' (p. 156). Although there is so much to say, Everard admits that '"Lucy does not talk to me"' (p. 160). Instead, she censors herself further, as 'the pleas there'd been, the certainty that this was what mattered most, everything so often repeated, the longing, the begging: word for word, spoken, written, all became a torment in Lucy's head while her father was silent and she was silent too' (p. 175). Her father's arrival is too late for Lucy's hopes of happiness as Ralph has married someone else: 'Lucy tried to say that she might have married the man she loved . . . but the words would not come' (p. 190). Her father 'had been aware of her jealousy of a wife; he knew it was less painful than it had been. But none of that was ever said' (p. 197).

Although his return signifies a progression, after thirty years the barriers to communication remain the same.

In *The Story of Lucy Gault*, even letters that arrive at their intended destination fail to arrive and therefore assist the censorship of Lucy. After the Gaults cannot be contacted, Sullivan attempts to write to other members of the family. After the multiple pathways of the post have failed him, he turns to the many branches of the family tree in order to locate his addressee. After failing to contact Everard's brother, he attempts to reach Heloise's aunt: 'the reply he received – from a Miss Chambré, companion to the lady who was an invalid – expressed horror, and distaste for what had occurred' (p. 58). Sullivan's attempts to explain inevitably lead to further misinterpretation as Lucy is again aligned with the horror of disobedience. His letter is intercepted by Miss Chambré, who insists that 'what was presently communicated [could not] be retailed to her employer' (p. 58). As Derrida suggests, 'all the precautions in the world are taken in vain, you can register your *envois* with a return receipt, crypt them, seal them, multiply coverings and envelopes, at the limit not even send your letter, still, in advance it is intercepted. It falls into anyone's hands.'[27] Through her influence over Heloise's relation, Miss Chambré 'believes the withholding of this most shocking news from an invalid is doubly justified' (p. 59). Therefore, even though the letter arrives, it fails to reach its addressee: 'even in arriving, the letter takes itself away *from the arrival at arrival*. It arrives elsewhere, always several times.'[28] Miss Chambré halts the letter's path because her employer's 'delicate heart might easily not sustain the strain of learning of such appalling thoughtlessness in a child' (p. 58). Lucy's disobedience positions her as an assumption to Miss Chambré, a further construction that ensures she is depicted as a horror. 'Mr Sullivan sighed over that. He might have pointed out, but did not do so, that Lucy Gault's conduct had spawned its own punishment' (p. 69). Later on in the text, even the news of Heloise's death cannot be delivered as

> Heloise's aunt had died herself. The Captain's letter was received by her long-time companion and the inheritor of her property and possessions. To Miss Chambré that a niece existed or did not was neither here nor there. She reread what had been written before

tearing the single sheet of paper into small, square pieces and dropping them into the fire. (p. 136)

Like the letters he did not send, Everard's attempts to communicate are thwarted, and as such the facts of death remain clouded. Uncannily, the characters in Trevor's text are uncertain who is dead and who is alive.

In addition to the multiple misplacements and interceptions in *The Story of Lucy Gault*, the contents of the letters are not satisfactory either to addressee or sender. Just as Miss Chambré refuses to pass on the tragic events to Heloise's aunt, writing fails to convey the message intended. As Derrida writes, 'within every sign already, every mark or every trait, there is distancing'.[29] Such frustration is experienced by Sullivan in his attempt to contact the authorities, as

the urgency he sought to convey in what he had written had clearly not registered. Nor did he trust the assurances he eventually received, but instead read into them an empty promise that was designed to soothe. Some garbled version of his pleas might one day be disseminated, stale by then and carelessly strung together, the poignancy of a family's agony reduced to nothing much. He imagined such a document filed away. (p. 60)

As Derrida suggests, 'letters are always post cards: neither legible nor illegible, open and radically unintelligible'.[30] Letters are revealed to be simultaneously cryptic and open, lacking the privacy assured by the postal service and coded through the dissemination of meaning associated with all signifiers. The urgency of the lawyer's position is not communicated through his use of language. Furthermore, Sullivan 'reads into' his replies 'empty promises designed to soothe', suggesting a concealed emptiness beneath the words received. Like the horrific misinterpretation of events, Sullivan's own depiction of those events becomes 'a garbled version'. As Derrida suggests in *For What Tomorrow*, it is 'because a letter can always not arrive at its destination that acts of deception (and other similar things – distraction and errors, multiple paths, complete misunderstandings, etc.) can suspend and hold at bay what you are calling the truth'.[31]

Just as the event of Lucy's disappearance is misread, language has its own potential to divert meaning and therefore is in constant movement itself. As Malabou writes of the sign, 'its destiny condemns it to travel, like a representative or missionary, in the place and stead of the instance that it is charged with designating'.[32] Therefore, if language itself travels, the possibility of a letter arriving is complicated by the non-arrival at signification: 'words of language in general already raise in and of themselves the question of displacement.'[33] Although a letter may arrive at its destination, the signification of that letter is undermined as the words themselves are in transit, leading to multiple pathways of miscommunication. As Malabou quotes from *The Post Card*, 'language poisons for us the most secret of our secrets'.[34] Through Lucy's interchange with her failed love Ralph, she remarks that 'afterwards, when she had posted it, she thought that [her] letter [to him] sounded false' (p. 137). As Derrida explores in *The Post Card*, love letters are the most private communications and yet remain simultaneously open to the other and closed to the intended recipient. He writes: 'I would like to address myself, in a straight line, directly, without *courrier*, only to you, but I do not arrive, and that is the worst of it. A tragedy, my love, of destination. Everything becomes a post card once more, legible for the other, even if he understands nothing about it.'[35] The privacy of the communication is undermined by the openness of the procedure of sending. As Lucy admits, her letter sounded false because language cannot articulate its intended meaning. In this way, language becomes a postal system, a courier that repeatedly sends its codes through a network of branching pathways. On rereading a reply from Ralph, she discovers 'a mood she had earlier missed, a meaning in statements and declarations that was imprecise, as if the wording had been reluctant to be otherwise' (p. 138). Although she receives her lover's communication, his words are tainted with imprecision, as if the words themselves were speaking and not Ralph. In this way, language is a poor medium for signification through its transitory role as courier.

In the end, Lucy acknowledges that 'all the letters in the world would not have made a difference' (p. 194) as letters and verbal communications are powerless to change a skewed pathway that leads a family lineage out of joint. As William Trevor's text has demonstrated, such an order is dislocated through misinterpretation, interception and catastrophe. As Trevor's title indicates, *The Story of Lucy Gault* highlights the narrative construction that she has become, suggesting that we ourselves construct most of the horrors we fear through miscommunication.

3

The Gothic Double Revised: Memory, Mourning and Illegal Twins in The Sea

୨୭

The double is a Gothic trope explored in a variety of texts that range from *Frankenstein* to Niffenegger's *Her Fearful Symmetry*. As a 'dark other', the double has functioned as a representation of the darker side of the self. This chapter revises this understanding of the double by exploring a twenty-first-century example of this classic Gothic theme. The revision explores the act of mourning a deceased other, a position which results in an ethical understanding of the self. Such an experience forces a renegotiation of the space of memory as a 'double stage',[1] highlighting the duality of the self through the ability to remember. This chapter explores the haunting nature of mourning as a return to the past, a disruption of linearity achieved through space and the screen of memory. Through the desire to revisit spaces of the past, a spectral pathway is produced, a route of memorial ruins that neither leads to a destination nor returns to an origin. Through the relationship between the mourner and the mourned, the relation of the individual to the dead other is evaluated to highlight the inaccuracy of memory. The consequence of interacting with dead others, an experience that threatens the memory of the dead other and highlights the reassuring role of the other in the identity of the self, will be the focus for this chapter.

The Sea is a torrent of pasts blended with the uncertain, ever-shifting present of Max Morden, a recently bereaved art historian who relocates to a seaside village, Ballyless, where he had spent his childhood holidays. Having lost his wife Anna, he is left with his daughter Claire to try to rebuild his life. After Anna's death, Max is drawn (alone) to Ballyless, the seaside village where a traumatic event changed his life and marked his entry into ethical under-standing. His travels suggest 'the trackless wastes of which I wander lost',[2] a wandering without arrival initiated by Anna's death. For Max, bereavement[3] generates an episode of reflection that leads him to Ballyless where he mourns his childhood friends, Chloe and Myles Grace, whose untimely death (as children they walked into the sea and were lost forever) returns to him in perpetual collision with a tentative present. As a 'work of mourning',[4] Max writes 'a Book of the Dead'[5] to comprehend these events, tracing the lost pathway of remembrance towards the ghosts of his past. In *Black Sun: Depression and Melancholia*, Julia Kristeva equates mourning with a kind of 'disenchantment that I experience here and now, cruel as it may be, which appears, under scrutiny, to awaken echoes of old traumas, to which I realise I have never been able to resign myself'.[6] The grief that Max experiences after the loss of his wife provokes past mournings to resurface. Instead of the appearance of a ghost that haunts, Max's mind is haunted as an archival space, as 'we carry the dead with us only until we die too' (p. 119). As Peter Goodrich explores in *Oedipus Lex*,

> the object of memory is not ... the corpse – which has in any event also disappeared or putrefied – nor is it the state or the various signs of being dead or discontinued. The object of memory is the recollection of disappearance, the deciphering of the myths, emblems, and clues, the relics, ruins, or remains of the passage of that which is passed on.[7]

Memory is understood as an endless pathway constituted by the ruins of experience, impressions that have been left on the screen of the mind. Through Max's memory, mental and physical experiences of space intersect in an interrogation of spatial zones. Max begins the mourning process by revisiting the Cedars Hotel (where he met the Grace twins as a child) as a means of stimulating memories created there. In this way, physical space acts as a stimulus for mental or memorial space, a rebuilding that occurs through remembrance.

As a bereaved man in his sixties, the past is the most important tense for Max, since the mourning present is intolerable and any possible future looks bleak. After an argument with his daughter, he curls up in a bed that was 'low and narrow, hardly more than a cot' (p. 68) as if attempting to regress into the comfort of childhood. By dismissing the present, he allows his mind to be haunted by the past, an archive conjured by space and memory. In this way, *The Sea* shifts between different times and spaces, continuously moving between the spectral past and mourning present. As he writes, 'they creak, this present gate, that past sign, to this day, to this night, in my dreams' (p. 13). Max's work of mourning involves a desire to be haunted, a conjuring of the dead through spaces of the past. As Derrida states, 'the living body is the space in which thoughts or ideal, autonomised entities are gathered, is it not itself the "body of ghosts"?'[8] The mind's ability to remember (or archive) permits the production of a catalogue of spectres, concealed until mourning encourages their resurfacing. As Derrida outlines in 'The pit and the pyramid',

> the image thus interiorised in memory is no longer *there*, no longer existent or present, but preserved in an unconscious dwelling, conserved without consciousness. Intelligence keeps these images in reserve, submerged at the bottom of a very dark shelter, like the water in a nightlike or unconscious pit, or rather like a precious vein at the bottom of the mine.[9]

Like the archive, memory is housed in a dark submerged realm suggesting a hidden stage of the mind. As in a pit, memories are maintained in darkness until mourning disturbs the dust in which they are submerged, and allows them to be re-membered. As Derrida elaborates in 'Plato's pharmacy', 'memory [is] an unveiling (re-)producing a presence from a re-memoration as the mere repetition of a monument'.[10] The unveiling of memory is achieved through repetition, through the pathway already encountered now re-encountered through its remaining ruins. Such duality suggests the conscious mind is haunted by a dark double that preserves what the conscious mind assumes to be lost. Therefore, as entry to this dark space of memory, mourning can be understood as a haunting, an embracing of the spectral in the mind. As Derrida states in *Archive Fever: A Freudian Impression*, the structure of the archive is *spectral*. It is spectral *a priori*: neither present nor absent 'in the flesh,' neither visible nor invisible, a trace always referring to another whose eyes can never be met, no more than those of Hamlet's father.[11]

To archive is to gather traces of the past, to linger with the spectral in a housing of remains. An archive is persistently haunted because its traces always refer back to that which no longer signifies in the present. As Derrida suggests, an archive involves a 'deposition in an *arkheion* (which can be an ark or a temple), the consignation in a place of relative exteriority'.[12] The demarcation of space can act as a complex archiving mechanism, holding histories and memories within a specific realm. As Derrida suggests, memories are deposited in space, left behind as a reminding remainder of the past and the future.

Max's work of mourning engages with archives of the past to assist a translation of the mourning present. However, Max is so comfortable in the past that he learns to live within the archive, retreating entirely from the present as his efforts to digest and expel[13] the memory of his lost loved ones fail. As Freud suggests in 'Mourning and melancholia', attempting to withdraw from the mourning process provokes a 'struggle that can be so intense that a turning away from reality ensues'.[14] For Max, reality becomes memorial in his undivided attention to the past. Kristeva remarks that in melancholia, 'everything has gone by, they seem to say, but I am faithful to those bygone days, I am nailed down to them, no revolution is possible, there is no future'.[15] Through mourning, Max has become fixed to the past like a monument, stationary in his undisputed allegiance to that which has gone. His fixation on his childhood friends suggests a debt to remembrance, but also a repudiation of teleology. Max's desire to return to the past represents a rejection of the future, a refusal to continue the line of time induced by the fear of dissolution. Because of his allegiance to the dead other, Max's engagement with the living other becomes limited and his sense of self confused.

As he is haunted both internally through memory and externally through space, Max is haunted twofold. The duality of Max's haunting is further established by his mourning both Anna and the Grace twins: 'they were twins. I had never encountered twins before, in the flesh, and was fascinated and at the same time slightly repelled' (p. 80). Max's conflicting response recalls Freud's notion of the uncanny,[16] a simultaneous attraction and repulsion to what is both familiar and unfamiliar. His response echoes René Girard's assertion that 'twins inspire a particular terror' in that they 'often display a single social personality'[17] and yet are individual subjects. The 'doubling, dividing and interchanging of the self'[18] situates twins as a terrifying curiosity. The Grace twins, however, are unusual in addition to being twins: Myles cannot speak and has webbed feet, and Chloe is cruel and heartless, amused by events such as watching grasshoppers boil 'in their own fat' (p. 116).

The spectral depiction of the twins in Max's memory further enhances the uncanniness evident in this novel of doubles. As discussed later, memory is a double stage, a simultaneous interiority and exteriority, a collection of ruins that are both present and absent, alive and dead, real and imaginative. Max remembers the twins as spectral, emphasizing memory's intricate link to spectrality. He describes Chloe as follows:

> She wore [her hair] in a pageboy style, with a fringe at the front overhanging her handsome, high-domed, oddly convex forehead – like, it suddenly strikes me, remarkably like the forehead of that ghostly figure seen in profile hovering at the edge of Bonnard's *Table in Front of the Window.* (p. 137)

It is through memory that Max can recollect Chloe, but this comes at a price. Max can only remember the dead as spectral as memory is a practice of spectrality. Just as the liminal figure haunts Bonnard's painting, Chloe is recalled as spectral, occupying a double position of presence and absence in Max's mind. As Derrida suggests in 'Plato's pharmacy', 'memory always therefore already needs signs in order to recall the non-present, with which it is necessarily in relation'.[19] Signs act as prompts in order to revive the buried scars of memory, to illuminate that which is in the dark. In this instance, the fringe of a painted ghostly figure acts as a trigger for Max's memory of Chloe.

Myles's muteness further enhances the duality and uncanniness of the twins: 'Myles had been mute from birth. Or rather simply, he had never spoken. The doctors could find no cause that would account for his stubborn silence' (p. 82). Because Myles cannot speak, Max imagines Mr and Mrs Grace were 'a little afraid of him. That is no wonder either. It must have been like living with an all too visible, all too tangible poltergeist' (p. 84). Because Myles is different he inspires fear. One reason for this is that 'he said nothing but he was never silent' as 'he made dry little clicking noises at the back of his throat' and 'one heard him breathe' (p. 83). In this way, Myles cannot be categorized as silent or mute as his existence refutes such oppositions. Instead, he represents an uncanny presence, an observer who communicates in an altogether other (and untranslatable) language. His breathing and guttural noises are his attempt to communicate, and yet those around him (except for Chloe) cannot understand his signs. 'Neither parent could do proper sign language, and spoke to Myles by way of an improvised brusque dumb-show' (p. 83). Although Myles cannot speak, he is still capable of communication: 'Myles emerged from the ferns again and knelt and picked a blade of grass and blew another reed note between his thumbs and waited . . . a moment later from far off came Chloe's answering call' (p. 127). He is also capable of using language: 'the slogan Myles scrawled in chalk on the gate posts and on the footpath outside the gate' (p. 234). Although he cannot speak, Myles can write. The failure to speak reinforces Myles's spectrality as an uncanny lack of communication renders him absent. As Derrida writes in *The Gift of Death*: 'once I speak I am never and no longer myself, alone and unique. It is a very strange contract – both paradoxical and terrifying – that binds infinite responsibility to silence and secrecy.'[20] By refusing to speak, Myles remains singular in his connection with Chloe as his secrecy binds him to her through an ethical responsibility of silence. Myles's muteness enables him to maintain his thoughts and ideas with her only: 'as soon as one speaks, as soon as one enters the medium of language, one loses that very singularity.'[21] Therefore, in order to remain 'manacled' to Chloe, Myles must remain outside speech: 'brother and sister were engaged in one of their private wordless contests, tussling and squirming, plucking at each other with pincer fingers and trying to kick each other's shins' (p. 110). As Levinas suggests in *Totality and Infinity*, the other is 'a language without teaching, a silent language, an understanding without words, an expression in secret'.[22] By avoiding speech, the twins can communicate without a language that permits 'the reduction of the Other to the same',[23] and maintain their unity.

Even before their mysterious death, Max's experience of Chloe's twin was as an absence: 'being alone with Myles was like being in a room which someone had just violently left' (p. 83). Such a sense of lack is due to experiencing Myles *without Chloe*. As 'one mind and two bodies' (p. 80) the twins are a complete entity only when together. Their sense of self and existence is determined through the other. This is also the case for Max: through the otherness of the Grace twins, he begins to understand his sense of self. Chloe's response to what it felt like to be a twin is '"like two magnets," she said, "but turned the wrong way, pulling and pushing"' (p. 81). This dual response recalls the uncanny, a simultaneous attraction and repulsion, a shifting between union and separation. Max remembers how 'we were watching a film in which two convicts from a chaingang made their escape still manacled together, and beside me Chloe stirred and made a muffled sound, a sort of laughing sigh. "Look," she whispered, "it's me and Myles"' (p. 81). Her identification with criminals highlights how, as two bodies and one mind, the twins are against the law. This is particularly relevant to their suicide, walking into the sea as if manacled, 'tied to each other, tied and bound' (p. 82). Their decision to end their life not only takes the law into their own hands, but creates an untimely event, a rupture in the linearity of time as children should not take their own lives or die before their parents.

Through his experiences with the Grace twins, Max is educated in ways that exceed his childhood and impact on him as an adult. As John Wild writes in his introduction to *Totality and Infinity*, 'according to Levinas, I find myself existing in a world of alien things and elements which are other than, but not negations of myself'.[24] Through the alterity of Myles and Chloe Grace, Max learns about himself and the ethics of existence. In his recollections of Chloe in particular, Max writes that

> There was another reason why she must be kept inviolate, unpolluted by too much self-knowledge or, indeed, too sharp a knowledge of me. This was her *difference*. In her I had my first experience of the absolute otherness of other people. It is not too much to say – well

it is, but I shall say it anyway – that in Chloe the world was first manifest for me as an objective entity. (pp. 167–8)

His friendship with the Grace twins induces an ethical education on living with others. As Derrida recounts in *The Gift of Death*, 'as soon as I enter into a relation with the absolute other, my absolute singularity enters into relation with his on the level of obligation and duty'.[25] By interacting with the other, the 'I' is no longer 'I', there is no more singularity. And yet the duality of learning from the other always means learning about the self, a selfish education that results in an enhanced sense of identity. Because Max's first experience of the other is a divided one through the two bodies and one mind of twins, the impact upon his own existence is also divided. Max observes that 'the philosophers tell us that we are defined and have our being through others' (p. 217). Hence his experience with the twins leads him to a fragmented sense of identity, an existence that lacks his own twin. Through her difference (and her tie to Myles), Chloe teaches Max about objectivity and existence: 'no one had yet been real in the way that Chloe was. And if she was real, so, suddenly, was I' (p. 168). Hence Max's understanding of his own identity is achieved through the reality of an other, Anna. Such a transition is evident through renaming: on remembering the first time his mother met Anna, he recalls her saying: '"Why does she keep calling you Max?" she hissed at me when Anna had gone to the counter to fetch a scone for her. "Your name is not Max."' In response to this, Max says simply: '"It is now."' (p. 210) A new sense of identity is achieved through both Anna and the twins' lives, and also through their deaths. For Max, Chloe 'was I believe the true origin in me of self-consciousness' (p. 168). Through Chloe, Max begins to understand his own existence.[26] Because Max has relied upon the other for his sense of self, his education leaves him simultaneously vulnerable and free.

In severing me from the world and making me realise myself in being thus severed, she expelled me from that sense of the immanence of all things, the all things that had included me, in which up to then I had dwelt, in more or less blissful ignorance. Before, I had been housed, now I was in the open, in the clearing, with no shelter in sight. (p. 168)

As Levinas suggests in *Totality and Infinity*, 'the presence of the Other, a privileged heteronomy, does not clash with freedom but invests it'.[27] Through the Grace twins, Max achieves a sense of freedom and release, a reassurance of the world as a realm of many others rather than the isolation of the 'I'. 'The strangeness of the Other, his irreducibility to the I, to my thoughts and my possessions, is precisely accomplished as a calling into question of my spontaneity, as ethics.'[28] Before meeting Chloe, Max had been housed securely in a realm of ignorance about difference and otherness. After meeting the Grace twins, Max is suddenly thrust into a world of insecurity, a world where identity and existence are fragmented. To describe this moment of transition, Max chooses the metaphor of the house. As philosophy's exemplar of representation,[29] the house symbolizes the foundations of Western thought, a doctrine based upon binary oppositions such as inside and outside. Being forced into an unsheltered clearing dissolves reassurances of security that have been maintained through language. No longer contained within a binary system, Max must adjust to a new state of being. He can now contemplate a space and relationships that cannot be determined through oppositions. Therefore, 'the relation with the Other is the only relation where such an overturning of formal logic can occur'.[30] For Levinas, our sense of self is achieved not through our security as a solitary being, but through interactions with others, relationships which frustrate the binary of self and other.

After he loses his wife, Max returns to the site of this understanding, hoping for the same reassurance from a memorial conjuring of the twins. He also desires their manacled togetherness and half-heartedly tries to copy their suicide by walking into the sea. After losing the others (Chloe, Myles, Anna) who had taught him so much, Max becomes like Myles: mute and spectral, and so attached to Chloe that he too will follow her into the sea. In the final moments before the twins end their lives, Max, Chloe and Myles break into a 'disused groundsman's hut' (p. 235). Inside, Chloe and Max begin to caress one another, educating one another sexually. Whilst doing so, Chloe reaches out for Myles's hand 'and clasped it' (p. 241). Chloe's sharing of intimate moments with her brother further suggests their connected sense of existence. At this moment, their governess Rose enters the hut and scolds Chloe while Myles, 'still sprawled on the bench beside me, gave a low laugh. I stared at him. It seemed to me that he had spoken' (p. 243). The unity of the three children is such that Max shares Myles's rare moments of speech, just as Chloe does. Hence, the decision of the Grace twins to walk into the sea (and leave him behind) traumatizes him for the rest of his life. As Levinas suggests in *Totality and Infinity*, 'the Other, inseparable from the very event of transcendence, is situated in the region from which death, possibly murder, comes'.[31] Without Chloe and Myles, Max's identity becomes fragmented, a state which is renewed after Anna's death: 'there are times . . . when I seem to know nothing, when everything I did know seems to have fallen out of my mind like a shower of rain' (p. 212). In mourning, Max dismisses the living other in favour of the dead. After the trauma of the loss of his significant others, Max closes down his ability to be with others, in particular his daughter Claire: 'she does not telephone because I have warned her I will take no calls, even from her' (p. 43). His failure of empathy results in his near suicide, as his sense of existence is shackled to dead others.

In a manacled state to those he has lost, Max experiences the uncanniness of union with the (dead) other. As Julia Kristeva suggests, 'melancholy persons settle the lost Thing or object within themselves, identifying with the loss's beneficial features on the one hand, with its maleficent ones on the other. This presents us with the first state of the self's doubling.'[32] After Anna's death, Max positions Anna within himself,[33] as in mourning he is manacled to his lost other. As he suggests, 'we carry the dead with us' (p. 119) in an attempt to preserve memory. Like Chloe and Myles who were 'one mind and two bodies' (p. 80), Max clings on to the memory of Anna in an attempt to preserve the scars of memory. As Derrida writes in dialogue with Elisabeth Roudinesco, 'mourning annuls the other. I take him upon me, and consequently, I negate or delimit his infinite alterity.'[34] By incorporating the other into the mourner, this otherness is cancelled out. In concern for the self, the mourner removes the other's otherness. After Anna's death, Max asks: 'how could you go and leave me like this, floundering in my own foulness, with no one to save me from myself?' (p. 196). This suggests that Max requires the other to liberate him from his own sense of disturbed identity. After her death, he must return to himself, and hence dismiss her alterity. Max admits that 'I know so little of myself, how should I think to know another? . . . what I found in Anna from the first was a way of fulfilling the fantasy of myself' (pp. 215–16). Like Chloe, Max uses the other to locate himself. As Derrida continues, 'the other must remain the other . . . if I take him into me as a part of me, and if, consequently, I "narcissise" this death of the other by a successful work of mourning, I annihilate the other, I reduce or mitigate his death'.[35] As Max writes, Anna 'is lodged in me like a knife and yet I am beginning to forget her' (p. 215). Although Anna is now a part of his being, Max has lost her otherness, and hence is beginning to forget her as an other. Like Chloe and Myles's 'manacles', Anna and Max are connected by a material metaphor: a knife wedged into his being aligns memory with a wound, a scarring of the self. As Max remembers his marriage to Anna, he recalls that 'even in our most savage fights we were only violently at play, like Chloe and Myles in their wrestling matches' (p. 217). The union with the other achieved through blood and marriage reassures the self, a re-assurance lost in death. Grief forces a return to the singular that results in a sense of loss, and hence Max inflicts damage on the other by insisting on her continued reassurance of his sense of self.

In his obsession with the dead, Max chooses to live in spaces associated with the past and his lost loved ones. In this way, place instigates the recollection of memories for Max to gather and archive in his mind. As Georges Perec writes in his book *Species of Spaces*,

> The resurrected space of the bedroom is enough to bring back to life, to recall, to revive memories, the most fleeting and anodyne along with the most essential. The coenesthetic certainty of my body in the bed, the topographical certainty of the bed in the room, these alone reactivate my memory, and give it an acuity and a precision it hardly ever has otherwise.[36]

By reoccupying space, memory is rebuilt. Max's visit to the Cedars Hotel, for example, is to reactivate a trigger to awaken the archived past in his memory. 'The room was much as I remembered it, or looked as if it was as I remembered, for memories are always eager to match themselves seamlessly to the things and places of a revisited past' (p. 148). His uncertainty reflects the inaccuracy of memory and therefore a disservice to the deceased other. Instead of memory ensuring the otherness of the other, its inaccuracy ensures that Max does not retain any true sense of those he has lost. Instead, they become what he desires them to be: reassurances of his own identity. His attempt to knit together the layers of spatial present and past suggests a desire for coherence and entirety, a need that cannot be fulfilled by the fragmented nature of memory. He writes that 'I was nervous of this moment, the moment when I would have to take on the house, to put it on, as it were, like something I had worn in another, prelapsarian life' (p. 156). Max's description of the hotel as clothing suggests that spaces are a part of the self, an interior exterior: we locate ourselves in space, and yet space is simultaneously worn, emitted as an outside. Like the screen of memory, the experience of the hotel is an inside outside. The hotel becomes a disappointment to Max when he realizes that

> Everything was slightly out of scale, all angles slightly out of true. The staircase was steeper, the landing pokier, the lavatory window looked not on to the road, as I thought it should, but back across the fields. I experienced a sense almost of panic as the real, the crassly complacent real, took hold of the things I thought I remembered and shook them into its own shape. (p. 156)

Max's experience of the Cedars Hotel is out of joint with his past and hence induces panic: unlike his forced placement of the other, the spaces of his past do not reassure him. The hotel in his memory and the hotel in reality have overlapped with one another in a perverse illustration of the malleability of space, as through the scars of memory space is distorted.

Max's mythic past appears to be comprised of constructions produced like paintings by 'applying a dab of colour here, scumbling a detail there', referring to memories of people or places as 'when I stand back to survey my handiwork' (p. 224). These creations, however, are destructive, as 'the result of all this close work is that my focus on them is blurred rather than sharpened' (p. 224), suggesting the inaccuracy of Max's recollections. Through this description of paintings, the memories of the Graces are aligned with screens, surfaces that signify through colour, light and dark: 'the image of her that I hold in my head is fraying, bits of pigments, flakes of gold leaf, are chipping off. Will the whole canvas be empty one day?' (p. 215). Such a representation highlights the violence of his remembering as he has depicted the other according to his wishes rather than the reality. As Derrida suggests in *Memoires for Paul de Man*, Max is experiencing 'a *possible mourning* which would interiorise within us the image, idol, or ideal of the other who is dead and lives only in us'.[37] Through the scarring of remembrance, memory retains the ideal of the other which is inaccurate and subjective. Memory and imagination are therefore bound together so tightly that Max cannot tell one from the other: 'if it is Memory herself who is at work here and not some other, more fanciful muse' (p. 163). Therefore, the impact of the death of the other is on the self. This failed ethical position suggests that Max correlates his suffering with himself, and hence that his memory has the potential to be unreliable as a self-reflection rather than an impossible ethics whose focus is the other.

For Max, the uncanniness of the Cedars Hotel is emphasized by the landlady, Miss Rose Vavasour. As witnesses to the death of the twins, he and Rose are thus bound together by shared memories: 'a certain formal distance is necessary for the good maintenance of the dainty relation we have forged, re-forged, between us over these past few weeks' (p. 261). In occupying the house, Rose is faithful to her memories and revisits the space that changed her life. In doing so, she, like Max, inhabits an archive of the past, and represents a remainder, a trace of the memories he so desperately seeks. Like Max, she has also taken on a new identity: throughout the text she is referred to as Miss Vavasour, and it is only towards the end of the text that Max reveals 'I do not think it means that I can call her Rose' (pp. 260–1). Although they are a key to his past, Max does not pursue their shared memories as 'the old unasked questions come swarming forward again' (p. 260). His silence regarding the death of the twins aligns him with the mute existence of Myles, Chloe's other who does not communicate through speech. It also suggests the disjointed nature of memory (and the selfishness of a supposed ethical mourning), as Rose's account of events may be 'out of scale' with Max's.

However, the hotel is not the only space that has changed. Max has not considered how he has also changed since he stayed there as a child. One possible explanation for the angles 'out of scale' or for the small size of the landing would be that Max has grown into a man since his stay at the Cedars. Like Alice in *Alice's Adventures in Wonderland*, Max's experience of disproportion leaves him feeling anxious, as the Cedars Hotel is structured by the supplemental re-collections that he holds in his mind. Even though all traces of the Graces have been removed, the space of their dwelling is enough to activate archived memories. However, there are fewer traces remaining than he had expected.

> It had retained hardly anything of the past, of the part of the past that I knew here. I had hoped for something definite of the Graces, no matter how small or seemingly insignificant, a faded photo, say, forgotten in a drawer, a lock of hair, or even a hair-pin, lodged between the floorboards, but there was nothing, nothing like that. No remembered atmosphere, either, to speak of. I suppose so many of the living passing through – it is a lodging house, after all – have worn away all traces of the dead. (p. 39)

Max is disappointed with this space because of its failure to supplement his own interpretation of the past. His hope for 'something definite of the Graces' is an attempt to reassure this interpretation, but those who have passed through the hotel have removed marks of the dead.[38]

Although Max is living in his own past, it is a past of his own construction and he is therefore recreating the events of his past in his attempts to remember them. As explored in *Archive Fever*, 'an event [Max's journey] is always *archiving* [Max's writings]. An event is an archiving act even if there may not be a "proper" archive and even if the archive of an event, as its interpretation, must always remain open.'[39] Therefore, the process of writing, or 'archivization, produces as much as it records the event'[40] as ultimately, memory is inaccurately informed by the imagination as well as the past. Like the supplement, the trace of the deceased in the realm of the living is dangerous and '*seductive*, it leads desire away from the good path, makes it err far from natural ways, guides it towards its loss or fall and therefore it is a sort of lapse or scandal'.[41] Like the trace, the supplement is a rupture, a fracturing of traditional systems experienced through the subjective nature of memory, a practice that leads one away from the real and into the realm of imagination. As Susan Sontag writes, the images of memory can be aligned with the photograph as 'not only an image, an interpretation of the real, it is also a trace, something directly stencilled off the real, like a footprint or a death mask'.[42] Although a subjective distortion of reality, the photographic nature of memory retains a trace of the real. Like images achieved through the burning of light (and shadows of the dark) onto paper, memories are stencilled on an outline of a burning event, although their accuracy is undermined by the shadows cast onto the screen of the mind.

Just as mourning results in a return to the Cedars Hotel, spaces such as the cinema retain traces of Max's time with the Grace twins. The memory of his first kiss with Chloe takes Max back to a picture-house, 'a barn-like structure set on a bit of scrubby waste-land' (p. 143):

> Chloe and I were sitting in the middle of a bench near the front, so close to the screen that it seemed to tilt out over us at the top and even the most benign of the black-and-white phantoms flickering across it loomed with a manic intensity. (p. 143)

In addition to the spectrality of memory, Derrida investigates how 'cinema is the art of phantoms, it is neither image nor perception'.[43] Cinematic spectrality consists of the reproduction of images that are secondary to actual events, dislocating the presence of the present. The filming of the film has already been done, the events have already occurred. In this sense, the cinema projects events in a fashion not dissimilar to how they are recalled in memory: 'above us the screen retained a throbbing grey penumbral glow that lasted a long moment before fading, and of which something seemed to remain even when it was gone, the ghost of a ghost' (p.143). The shadow that remains is an echo of what was and therefore has been distorted in some way. Traditionally, screens such as paper have been used by philosophy to secure signification through language. In this text, however, the screen of the mind is unreliable, subject to distortions, and holds traces with no referent. Shadows of memory suggest outlines with no content or (traditional) signification. Therefore, remembrance is remembered through a screen that obscures as much as it recalls.

Like the photograph, memory is achieved through the impressions of light and dark upon a screen resulting in the shadow of an image, a silhouette of a moment captured. As Roland Barthes writes in *Camera Lucida*, photography 'is a wound'[44] produced through a *punctum*: a 'sting, speck, [a] little hole' that is 'lightning like',[45] a 'floating flash'.[46] The light that permits photography marks the paper as memory scars the mind, an action which suggests the violence of the mourner towards the memory of the deceased other. The impression that remains in the memory is one of death, as 'everything which happens within the frame dies absolutely once this frame is passed beyond'.[47] The moment is captured and becomes a trace of that moment, not the moment itself. Memory is caught through time, marking its death as it does so as 'in every photograph [there is] the return of the dead'.[48]

As Gideon Ofrat writes in *The Jewish Derrida*, 'any memory is a kind of ruin, writes Derrida, as it constitutes something that was and is no longer'.[49] Because there can be no successful mourning, the loss of loved ones results in an incorporation of the dead within ourselves, an incorporation which inevitably distorts the other. As Derrida suggests in *Memoires for Paul de Man*, 'memory stays with traces, in order to "preserve" them, but traces of a past that has never been present, traces which themselves never occupy the form of presence and always remain, as it were, to come – come from the future, from the *to come*'.[50] The traces that remain in memory are for the future because they remain at the disposal of the one who remembers them. Hence, the traces of memory remain for the remem-berer to adapt and re-vision in the future, they signify a future signifi-cation, a re-membering that is always to come. Such markings of the traces are 'the opening of the first exteriority in general, the enigmatic relationship of the living to its other and of an inside to an outside'.[51] In this way, the screen of memory acts as a hymen between realms, a transparent wall demonstrating the trace of the other in the same, the inside within the outside. The 'hymen as protective screen'[52] stands between the inner crypt and an exteriority, 'located between present acts that don't take place. What takes place is only *entre*, the place, the spacing, which is nothing.'[53] Like the terms 'trace', *différance* and *pharmakon*, the hymen escapes 'philosophical mastery' and 'admit[s] into [its] games both contradiction and noncontradiction'.[54] By resisting penetration, translation or signification, the screen of traces enacts 'a *double scene* upon a double stage. It operates in two absolutely different places at once.'[55] Simultaneously other and self, inside and outside, fact and fiction, the memory as screen never allows the mourner to mourn successfully. Instead, memories refer back to an origin that never was, an event that can never be traced, to a path of 'trackless wastes of which I wander lost' (p. 24).

Fixation on memory and dead others has an immense impact upon the being of the mourner. After Anna's death, Max becomes more alert to the sensations of his own body as testament to his being alive. 'It is as if I were being tested for vital signs, for signs of feeling, for signs of life' (p. 42). He goes on to note how

> I have developed too a queasy fascination with the processes of my body, the gradual ones, the way for instance my hair and my fingernails insistently keep growing, no matter what state I am in, what anguish I may be undergoing. It seems so inconsiderate, so heedless of circum-stance, this relentless generation of matter that is already dead. (p. 70)

His continued reliance upon the other for reassurance results in an alignment with the spectral, as through the impact of the dead other Max begins to reinterpret his own body. Clearly, the reassurance he so desperately seeks from the dead other is not being provided. Because he is persistently haunted, he begins to understand himself as a ghost. A glance in the mirror reveals he has 'definitely something of the look of a hanged man ... not yet hanged perhaps but definitely on Death Row' (pp. 128–9). By depicting himself as a man on Death Row, Max demonstrates his focus towards a death-to-come. In Max's recollections, he begins to see himself as an absence.

> I had a sudden image of myself as a sort of large dark simian something slumped there at the table, or not a something but a nothing, rather, a hole in the room, a palpable absence, a darkness visible. It was very strange. I saw the scene as if from outside myself ... and I this big dark indistinct shape, like the shape that no one at the séance sees until the daguerreotype is developed. I think I am becoming my own ghost. (p. 193)

The division of Max's sense of self begins with unease about his existence and develops into understanding himself as a ghost. His remembered response to the twins' death is moving 'among the rooms as if I were myself a thing of air, a drifting spirit, Ariel set free and at a loss' (p. 247). Like the experience of being with Myles ('being in a room someone had just violently left'), Max has now become an absence; his spectralization occurs immediately after the death of the twins. After finding out Anna's illness is terminal, a 'pit opened under our feet that day in Mr Todd's rooms' (p. 93). As Julia Kristeva suggests, it is 'on the frontiers of life and death [that] occasionally I have the arrogant feeling of being witness to the meaninglessness of Being, of revealing the absurdity of bonds and beings'.[56] On the threshold of life, Max's melancholic perspective is that his existence is crumbling around him. Freud's essay 'Mourning and melancholia' suggests that melancholia is 'a profoundly painful dejection, abrogation of interest in the outside world, loss of the capacity to love, inhibition of all activity' containing 'self-reproaches' and 'delusional expectation of punishment'.[57] Aligned with mourning, melancholia is associated with a mental state of depression that arises after mourning. Such a state is induced by the death of the reassuring other. Max's impression of a condemned man on Death Row is his punishment for surviving whilst Anna has died: 'the survivor's guilt . . . without fault or debt, it is, in truth, an *entrusted responsibility*.'[58] Without the reassurance of the other, Max's ethical responsibility is to negate his own existence in a mourning that can never be successful.

After mourning, Max's existence is problematic as he can no longer rely upon oppositions to distinguish himself from the dead. Therefore, *The Sea* reveals how complex the mourning subject can be. As Derrida explores in *Specters of Marx*, 'I am' becomes 'I am haunted: I am haunted by myself'[59] as to live is to house (archive) memorial hauntings in the space of the mind. This is further evident when Max has a dream about a typewriter: 'I was trying to write my will on a machine that was lacking the word *I*. The letter *I*, that is, small and large' (p. 71). It is thus impossible for Max to compose a will,[60] a word containing the letter 'I'. It also suggests an inability to express himself as a coherent 'I', reaffirming his mourning state. His fear that the letter 'I' is removed suggests an insecurity that he cannot articulate himself, that everything around him (including the typewriter itself) will become infected with the absence that plagues him wherever he turns. In this way, the letter 'I' has been erased just as he has been erased by his own memories, as by living in the past, Max is no longer a signifying subject. Through mourning, Max has become Chloe's other, the spectral Myles who cannot signify through speech. By revisiting the Cedars, Max recalls how

> standing with Mrs Grace in that sunlit living room, or sitting with Chloe in the dark of the picture-house, I was there and not there, myself and revenant, immured in the moment and yet hovering some-how on the point of departure. (p. 98)

Max's sense of self is doubled by his continuing existence in the past and the present. In this way, he haunts himself, he has become his own ghost. Like the photograph, Max is fixed in time to the past, but always on the point of movement towards the present. In *Memoires for Paul de Man*, Derrida poses the question: 'what if there were a *memory of the present* and that far from fitting the present to itself, it divided the instant?'[61] The idea of the instant is divided for Max as he occupies different times and spaces simultaneously.

The melancholia Max experiences is so extreme that he considers suicide in a sinister replication of the twins walking into the sea. Therefore, Max seeks penance by moving to the site of the Grace twins' death at Ballyless. His drunken re-enactment of their death is 'not a disguised act of war but a merging with sadness and, beyond it, with that impossible love, never reached, always elsewhere, such as the promises of death'.[62] The oblivion offered by the sea's expanse provides an opportunity for forgetfulness, while replicating the act of suicide reunites him with his deceased friends. In the *Politics of Friendship*, Derrida proposes that 'to love in love or friendship would always mean: I can kill you, you can kill me, we can kill ourselves. Therefore, in all cases, we *already* are dead for one another.'[63] As Levinas explores, looking at the other is to engage with death, theirs and mine. In doing so, the living can make the ultimate sacrifice by identifying individual existence with the death of all others. The resolution Max achieves is accomplished by the realization that he is willing to die for the others he has lost. Losing his footing foils his attempt at suicide, knocking him unconscious by striking his 'temple on a stone' (p. 254). In his attempt to die for the other, Max is saved from himself by a guest at the Cedars referred to as the 'Colonel'. Max recalls how 'I do not remember the Colonel finding me, although he insists I spoke to him quite sensibly, and allowed him to help me up and walk me back to the Cedars' (p. 254). His near-death experience revives Max's interest in others that surround him and he renews his relationship with his daughter Claire, allowing her to become the other that he relies on. The rescue reaffirms an ethical reliance on living others, and Max's identity becomes less fragmented. After recovering from his injuries, he is informed by his daughter that he must 'let her take me home where she will care for me' (p. 259). After turning towards death, Max returns to an existence that is dependent on living others rather than dead others.

After his double loss, Max feels that he is 'learning to live amongst the living again' (p. 192). Derrida states how 'the time of the "learning to live"' amounts to learning to 'live *with* ghosts. In any case from the other at the edge of life'.[64] Max is learning to live with ghostly, inadequate memories, but also with knowledge that destabilizes oppositions, celebrates the double and the simultaneous. As the narrative comes to an end, Max recalls another moment in Ballyless when

> the whole sea surged, it was not a wave, but a smooth rolling swell that seemed to come up from the deeps, as if something vast down there had stirred itself, and I was lifted briefly and carried a little way toward the shore and then was set down on my feet as before, as if nothing had happened. (p. 264)

This memory enters Max's mind at exactly the right time. Faced with the death of his wife, he recalls the sea as an escape into oblivion, a return to a past trauma in search for atonement. For him, resolution is achieved through the insignificant: 'indeed nothing had happened, a momentous nothing, just another of the great world's shrugs of indifference' (p. 264). Like the missing key on his typewriter, the insignificant signifies for Max by opening his mind to the future. After this recollection, a 'happy lightsomeness' appears before him: 'it was as if I had stepped suddenly out of the dark into a splash of pale, salt-washed sunlight' (p. 26). Through this realization, Max learns to live amongst the living, with the shadows of the dead at his side.

4

Conjuration, Digestion, Expulsion: The Law of Mourning in The Gathering

 co

This chapter examines the ritual of mourning as a process that firstly conjures, then digests, and finally expels. As such, the tradition of mourning ensures the progression of the body and soul of the deceased. In Anne Enright's text, the legal importance of this process – in which mourners are required to gather together to ensure its success – is clear.

Narrated by the protagonist, Veronica, *The Gathering* records the impact of death on the Hegarty family. Through the process of mourning, Enright's text demonstrates how the ritual of death is intimately connected to the law and the architecture of the house. Veronica's experience of her family home is distorted after the loss of a sibling whose ghost demands the truth, the revelation of a secret. In addition to his ghost, the body of Veronica's brother Liam also invades the family home by 'lying in state'[1] and in doing so disturbs thresholds and spatial boundaries. Hence the protagonist is haunted by both spirit and body. Liam's body is a welcomed guest in the household, whilst his ghost simultaneously arrives as an uninvited guest. A corpse in a space occupied by the living is disruptive of the spatial boundaries and security of the home, and yet, through the ritual of mourning, the body is welcomed in order to expel or lay to rest. Such mourning, however, is impossible: the expulsion is unsuccessful as the mourner internalizes the dead within a memorial crypt. As Derrida writes in *For what Tomorrow,*

mourning *must* be impossible. Successful mourning is failed mourning.
In successful mourning, I incorporate the one who has died, I assimilate
him to myself, I reconcile myself with death, and consequently, I deny
death and the alterity of the dead other and of death as other. I am
therefore, unfaithful.[2]

Mourning is not a process as such a journey can never begin. Although
the law insists upon it, mourning can never expel the dead other.

Although Liam's suicide is not illegal,[3] the law is intimately involved
in his death. For Liam to be certified dead, his sisters must find
records to confirm his identity. 'Kitty [ran] around London and me
around Dublin for dental records, his height, and the colour of his
hair, and the tattoo on his right shoulder.'[4] The law's desire to control
the ritual of death is rather problematic, as like the ghost, 'the law
is nothing that is present'.[5] A crime committed against Liam (child
abuse), which remained unpunished, highlights the law's inadequacy.
Like the corpse, 'any crime, because it draws attention to the fragility
of the law, is abject'.[6] In determining the line between criminality
and legality, the law is a controlling mechanism achieved through
the imposition (and guarding) of boundaries, a position akin to the
role of the house in philosophy. As Mark Wigley suggests: 'the question
of the law of the house is, after all, that of the status of law itself.
The law is never more than domestic.'[7]

After Liam's death, Veronica remarks that 'I should start at the
place where Liam walked into the sea – because there is an order
to these things that has to be obeyed' (p. 76). Veronica's language of
mourning is determined by the law through an obligation to act
according to a preconceived set of rules. In this way, mourning is
determined by legality. Her narrative begins with the assertion that
'I need to bear witness to an uncertain event' (p. 1). Her desire to
testify for her brother relates her story to the official channels of
the law and the achievement of some form of justice. She elaborates
to state that 'you can not libel the dead, I think, you can only console
them' (p. 2). The law attempts to control the articulation of the dead
through language: 'at the very least, to be dead means that no profit
or deficit, no good or evil, whether calculated or not, can *ever return
again* to the bearer of the name.'[8] The law dictates that the dead are
not responsible for any crimes, as they are excluded as outlaws: 'the

law is a space, a kind of interior, such that to break the law is to be "outside" it, an outlaw'.[9] And yet even the excluded remains under the control of the excluder.[10]

As explored elsewhere in this book, the law is an absent present force that originates with text. As Derrida writes in 'Freud and the scene of writing', 'the metaphor of writing which haunts European discourse [is] the repression of writing as the repression of that which threatens presence and the mastering of absence'.[11] Like the law's depiction of itself as a presence, the written words of the law are unstable and vulnerable to interpretation. Derrida takes this further in *Acts of Religion*: 'law is essentially *deconstructible*, whether because it is founded, that is to say constructed, upon interpretable and transformable textual strata or because its ultimate foundation is by definition unfounded'.[12] Therefore, the origin of law is profoundly uncertain and responds by attempting to make itself present through the medium of paper. 'The origin of writing is refusal – denial, Otherness. Law and authority demand and expect the similar, the same. Concretizing the law (in the original speech) in writing is condemned to Otherness.'[13] Because the law insists on the textual, it is already open to the other, vulnerable to interpretation through a perverse hospitality which enables the other to enter and occupy it. Just as hospitality is simultaneously an authorization and a refusal, writing is also contradictory as a record open to interpretation. As Western (Judaeo-Christian) law originates from the Ten Commandments inscribed in stone, the law has always depended upon writing. As Peter Goodrich writes in his book *Oedipus Lex*: 'the Decalogue was presented in the forbidding and erased form of Commandments inscribed in stone and also pitched dramatically against idols, false images, or other gods.'[14] Through its potential for further erasure (as indicated by Moses's erasure of the Ten Commandments) the demise of the law began with the written word. Due to this, the presence of the law is even more obscure. In his essay 'Before the law', Derrida examines Kafka's story of the same title, a narrative representing a path that (ultimately) never leads to the law.

It seems that the law as such should never give rise to any story. To be invested with its categorical authority, the law must be without history, genesis, or any possible derivation. That would be *the law of the law* . . . narrative accounts would try to approach the law and make it present, to enter into a relation with it, indeed, to enter it and become *intrinsic* to it, but none of these things can be accomplished.[15]

The law can provide no pathway for itself as there is no destination for the narrative to lead to, and no arrival to permit access. As no site can be located, the law is spectral: 'there is some law, some law which *is not there but which exists*'.[16] The law contradicts itself by instructing from nowhere: 'the law is silent . . . We do not know what it is, who it is, where it is. Is it a thing, a person, a discourse, a voice, a document, or simply a nothing that incessantly defers access to itself.'[17] This deferral of presence allows the law to remain elusive and unlocatable. Like religious idols, the law exerts its power without being seen. 'It is the origin of literature at the same time as the origin of law – like the dead father, a story told, a spreading rumor, without author or end, but an ineluctable and unforgettable story . . . the law is even more frightening and fantastic, *unheimlich* or uncanny.'[18] The law is uncanny because it is persistently familiar as a provider of the rules of existence. And yet it is also unfamiliar as a present absence that positions itself everywhere, whilst being found nowhere: 'the apparent world of the law, like the ecclesiastical order of images from which it devolved, is only ever an *indicium*, a symptom or sign of the value of law and of that metaphysical or invisible order that extends beyond or underpins the tangible service realm of legal instruments and judgements.'[19] Like a spectre,[20] the law operates as a symbol of itself which governs in place of an attendance that cannot be located.

Through her interaction with the law via her brother's death, Veronica realizes that the release of his body depends upon the law's approval.

What else am I to make of the 10 days we have to wait for paperwork, the death certificates and removal orders, that will have to find their separate ways into the one envelope that will accompany my brother on his journey home. Meanwhile, as computers wait and printers jam, as coroner's assistants go to the gym, and registrars wrestle with the collapse of their central heating systems, Liam lies in some unspecified foreign fridge. (p. 182)

As Liam has died in England and his family live in Ireland, the final journey of the body is delayed by the necessary legal paperwork that must accompany it. Hence, travelling along with the body of Liam is a body of papers relating to the official certification of death, as recorded and produced by the invisible hand of the law. The purpose of such papers is that death must be pronounced, the body must be spoken for. The absence induced by a corpse is counteracted by the weight of documentation, a significant body of paper that forces the corpse to signify through the discourse of the law. As Derrida writes in *Paper Machine*: 'paper will continue to hold a sacred power. It has the force of law, it gives accreditation, it incorporates, it even embodies the soul of the law, its letter and its spirit.'[21] Like the Ten Commandments, the written is useless without the support of a substance to hold it. '*Biblion* then, would only mean "writing paper", and not book, nor oeuvre or opus, only the substance of a particular support – bark.'[22] Paper assists the law in providing it with presentation, and a manifestation of presence. Like the wood of the coffin that supports Liam's corpse, the paper supports the official recognition of death. Like Freud's 'Mystic Writing Pad', 'it is a return to the ancient method of writing upon tablets of clay or wax: a pointed stilus scratches the surface, the depressions upon which constitute the "writing"'.[23] The force of the instrument on the pad induces signification through the impressions left behind. 'Paper often became the place of the self's appropriation of itself, then of becoming a subject in law.'[24] Although avoiding the law's involvement in the crimes committed against him as a child, Liam cannot resist the force of the law in his death. Just as birth is recorded and regulated, the relation between the law and death is deeply uncanny. In the moment of tragic loss for a family, the law steps in as the ultimate uncanny guest, uninvited, yet permitted through the law of law. The law grants itself permission to enter the home, and yet it can only do so as a guest.

As Gideon Ofrat writes: 'this pairing of violence and law thus guarantees deconstruction, the law's self-destruction. At the very heart of the law, says Benjamin, the rot is at work ... the law defends itself by means of violence that demolishes the law from within.'[25] As Ofrat writes, rot is 'at work' which permits the operation of the law while providing the potential for its disintegration. In an effort to secure its presence by founding itself upon text, the law encourages its own self-destruction. As Benjamin states, the central 'heart' or 'hearth' of the law is decaying, remaining only through a few fragile cinders of language. In his research on the occupation of the lawyer in the sixteenth and seventeenth centuries, Peter Goodrich states that lawyers would suffer extreme fatigue, but also a foul smell,[26] a sensation arising from the process of reading. As Derrida suggests: 'there is something decayed or rotten in law, which condemns it or ruins it in advance. Law is condemned, ruined, in ruins, ruinous.'[27] Inscribed with the ruins of text that attempt to secure all laws, the governing body of the law becomes rotten. Such imagery of decay originates with the decomposition of the weight of paper that the law depends upon. Like architecture, the law has been secured over an insecure ground: 'structure becomes erected by its very ruin, held up by what never stops eating away at its foundation.'[28] Therefore, the law is depicted as a rotting corpse. As Wigley suggests: 'everywhere, the tradition carries out its work of consumption behind the disguise of detachment, consuming what it claims to detach itself from.'[29] By commanding exclusion, the law simultaneously determines and houses the outlaw, controlling but also including the excluded within its own identity.

The Gathering begins with the crossing of a threshold as Veronica's mother opens the door of the family home to allow Veronica to enter. This moment demonstrates the conflicting nature of hospitality in its interactions with mourning. After she is permitted entry, Veronica's work of mourning begins with the delivery of Liam's death: 'I do my duty, which is to tell one human being about another human being, the few and careful details of how they met their end' (p. 8). Just as the threshold must be crossed in mourning, the death of her brother is described as a border crossing between land and sea: 'he finally walked away from us all into the sea' (pp. 155–6). In this way, the law has secured the moment of death as a movement across a border. As Gideon Ofrat writes: 'the borderline nature of death [acts] as transit point to that which lies beyond the border. The reference is to the line of demarcation between the possible and the impossible, between finite and infinite, between known and unknown.'[30] After crossing this border, Liam remains in a state of simultaneous exclusion and inclusion.

Liam's death must be delivered to his mother by Veronica, as she is the one who 'loved him most' (p. 11). Veronica is an *arrivant*, the bearer of loss under the guise of visitor. In delivering the news, she gives her mother the gift of death. As Derrida writes in his book of the same title: 'what is given in this trembling, in the actual trembling of terror, is nothing other than death itself, a new significance for death, a new apprehension of death, a new way in which to give oneself death or to put oneself to death.'[31] By providing such devastating information, Veronica takes on a liminal existence and becomes an uninvited guest, a position that aligns her with the spectre of her brother. This experience of the threshold is an extremely uncomfortable one as her mother says: '"come in. Come in", as she stands in the doorway, and does not move to let me pass' (p. 4). Her mother's words offer hospitality and yet her body reveals a rather different response. Instead of moving aside to welcome her guest, she remains where she is, blocking the entrance to the house and to hospitality. The complex relationship between the host and the guest is discussed in *Of Hospitality*, where Derrida observes that 'the Latin "hostis" means "guest" but also "enemy"'.[32] The vulnerability of the home to the other results in uncanniness as 'hospitality is the deconstruction of the at-home'.[33] The breaching of the habitat must be met with politeness (due to the law of hospitality) and yet with the guest comes the uncanny. To return to Derrida, 'the host thus becomes a retained hostage, a detained addressee, responsible for and victim of the gift'.[34] Just as Veronica provides her mother with the gift of death after crossing the threshold, her mother becomes hostage to Veronica's arrival. From the moment the visitor enters, the host is under her authority, as the host is now prisoner in his own home. 'It is *as if* the stranger or foreigner held the keys'[35] as the possession of keys indicates power, ownership and command of the property. Like the mourners that line the staircase after Veronica's grandfather dies, the other has mastery over the home: 'there was something tripping and wrong about this other ladder, made of shin-bones in support tights, at cross purposes to the staircase we were trying to climb' (p. 60). To allow the strange into the home is both a necessity and an immense vulnerability: 'a cultural or linguistic community, a family or a nation, cannot fail at the very least to suspend if not to betray this principle of absolute hospitality: so as to protect a "home", presumably, by guaranteeing property and "one's own" against the unrestricted arrival of the other.'[36] The law defines property as both secure and open, a contradiction which unsettles the privacy of the home. Like the conflicting experience incited by the other, the contradiction between privacy and property is one of many that will run through this chapter.

As Derrida writes, 'the law of hospitality, the express law that governs the general concept of hospitality, appears as a paradoxical law, pervertible and perverting'.[37] The right to hospitality is a conflicted one, as it perverts the law of the domestic. If hospitality is a right exercised via the force of the law, then that law is contradicted (perjured) by the space of the home. The law controls movement between thresholds and is founded on a threshold itself, being frequently referred to as a line that cannot be crossed. Yet hospitality demonstrates that the law refuses entry to itself: although it insists on hospitality, it refuses to be hospitable. Like the ability of the house to conceal its secrets, the distortion of the law of hospitality occurs inside the house as this is the source of the uncanny. It is the hidden nature of the home (the ability to achieve privacy and security) that threatens the law. The perversion of the law through hospitality relates to the abject, as outlined by Julia Kristeva: 'it is thus not lack of cleanliness or health that causes abjection but what disturbs identity, system, order. What does not respect borders, positions, rules. The in-between, the ambiguous, the composite.'[38] Due to the conflicting edict of hospitality, in the face of the guest the law becomes abject. After persistent exclusion of outlaws (achieved through a rule of thresholds), hospitality casts the law out of its own doctrines, whilst simultaneously being caught within them.

The ghost is the most uninvited guest as permission is neither required nor granted.[39] The ghost makes itself host as it crosses the threshold, and yet ghosts maintain a status as foreign, parasitical: 'the outsider inhabits a world of the half-living and of the dead.'[40] Unlike the body, the ghost cannot be excluded as it does not occupy space in a traditional sense. Like the position of outlaw, the ghost is simultaneously inside and outside. Therefore, the foreigner is aligned with the spectral, as both have the ability to disturb the boundaries of philosophy's paradigm of representation: the house. As explored in *Of Hospitality*, death does not visit '*of a place that no longer maintains its sovereignty. A place that is split, surrounded, divided, a haunted place.*

"A place of haunting", as he will specify, "is a place with no phantoms. Ghosts haunt places that exist without them, they return to where they have been excluded from."'[41] The ghost assumes a parasitical role and enters where unwelcome, as that which is excluded persistently returns.

Like many laws, the crime of trespass punishes the crossing of a threshold. 'Without this right [of asylum, hospitality] a new arrival can only be introduced "in my home", in the host's "at home", as a parasite, a guest who is wrong, illegitimate, clandestine, liable to expulsion or arrest.'[42] This is another example of the perverted law of hospitality as the crossing of the threshold is unwelcome and the trespasser is excluded. As Peter Goodrich suggests, the law is

> a symbolic permutation or point of passage between one order and another and it is variously depicted as hinge, Pleat, or gate, Mercury or Janus, name or text. It is the point of splitting or moving from one order to another, and intangible folding or exchange between different realms, changing places.[43]

Although the law dictates how thresholds should be utilized, the law describes itself as a threshold. From an uncertain abyssal origin, the law attempts to produce a foundation on a threshold space vulnerable to crossings. 'Law stands on the boundary between knowing and being. Law, both in its spiritual and temporal uses, its psychoanalytic and positive forms, marks the hinge, the breakage, between inside and outside, power and truth.'[44] Hence, the law is intimately bound by thresholds which leave it vulnerable to interpretation.

As Liam's ghost demonstrates, the privacy of the house is challenged by a desire for openness as he demands the revelation of child abuse. As a child Liam had suffered sexual abuse inflicted by his grandmother's friend and lover Nugent: 'I don't even know what name to put on it. I think you might call it a crime of the flesh' (p. 1). The crime that was committed results in a sense of injustice against the deceased. As the sole witness to these events, Veronica is the only one who can reveal the truth, and yet in doing so, she must challenge the privacy of the house by opening it up to interpretation. Liam's desire for the truth is assisted by the knowledge that he has a son, Rowan, who is revealed at the funeral: 'I look down, for the first time, at my brother's son' (p. 242). Because he has an heir, Veronica is compelled to tell the truth, as she owes it to Rowan's memory of his father. The absence created by Liam's death is reaffirmed by the presence of the small boy who will carry on his father's legacy. At the funeral, Veronica remarks how 'everyone wants to touch him' (p. 246). In the absence of Liam's body, there is now a presence with an uncanny resemblance to his father.[45]

To deliver the truth to her family regarding the possible motive for Liam's suicide, Veronica desires an impossible justice for Liam. The abuse he suffered as a child has a clear impact on his life, resulting in alcoholism, multiple failed relationships and suicide by drowning. It is, however, only Veronica who sees Liam's ghost, and only Veronica who is the subject of his gaze.

> There is a slumberous menace about his ghost that makes me realise how indifferent he was when he finally walked away from us all into the sea. I can feel his gaze on the skin of my cheek as he turns to look at me, uncanny and dead. I know what it is saying. The truth. The dead want nothing else. It is the only thing that they require. (pp. 155–6)

The persistent haunting of his sister is a demand for the truth and a justice unrelated to the law as 'law is deconstructed in the name of justice'.[46] For Liam, justice (in the legal sense) is impossible as he is dead, yet through the power of the spectral gaze he can communicate. Such a gaze is unlike a living gaze which is monitored by the law. Instead, the spectral gaze is beyond the law. As Derrida writes in *Specters of Marx*, 'we feel ourselves observed, sometimes under surveillance by it even before any apparition. Especially – and this is the event, for the specter is *of* the event – it sees us during a *visit*. It (re) pays us a visit. Visit upon visit, since it returns to see us'.[47] Just as the other becomes guest through visitation, the ghost repeatedly visits, and in doing so, repeatedly watches with a gaze that attempts to communicate.

As the man who committed the abuse, their grandmother[48] and the victim are dead, the law is powerless to act in relation to the crime committed against Liam. Therefore the spectre does not require the law; he demands something else. As Derrida writes in *A Taste for the Secret*, 'how can present beings which are out of joint, render justice? . . . how can one give what one does not have? Which is to say: how can that which is disadjusted render justice, or, more precisely, jointure'.[49] Neither the living nor the dead can achieve justice as it is not present to be 'given': 'one cannot speak *directly* about justice, thematise or objectivise justice . . . without immediately betraying justice, if not law'.[50] To articulate justice within language is to associate it irrevocably with the force of law, and yet, the entire notion of justice is unrelated to force. Because the operation of justice requires interpretation and a calculation according to set codes, the law's understanding of justice is a paradoxical one. 'For a decision to be just and responsible, it must, in its proper moment if there is one, be both regulated and without regulation: it must conserve the law and also destroy it or suspend it enough to have to reinvent it in each case.'[51] In this way, the spectre challenges the law and attempts to undo the thresholds that constitute it. Liam's spectral gaze thus demands the unspeakable from his sister: 'I know what I have to do – even though it is too late for the truth, I will tell the truth' (p. 259). However, despite her persistent concern with this revelation, Veronica cannot articulate it: the truth never arrives. Like the impossible nature of mourning that results in internalization of the deceased, Veronica never reveals the horror of the unspeakable secret.[52] Just as she does not expel her brother through the mourning process, neither does she eject the truth by expressing the horror of the secret abuse.

After Liam's death, Veronica's husband Tom encourages her to work[53] to distract her from the loss of her brother: 'this week's property supplement – Tom's little offering on the kitchen table – had a house for sale on Ada's Street' (p. 238). Like her brother Ivor who responds to mourning by considering purchasing a country house, Veronica is compelled to work through her mourning and seek revenge architecturally. Because she cannot voice the abuse of her brother, her expression of the unspeakable secret is only achieved spatially. As Tom's actions demonstrate, the space of the house is intimately connected to the experience of mourning. His offering to his bereaved wife is a newspaper that advertises houses. Her interest in the property supplement, however, is limited to experiences of the past: 'I could stalk it, Ada's house. I could buy this house up the road, and make it over, and sell on, until the day comes – not too far away, I feel sure – when I am standing in Ada's front room, pulling up a corner of the wallpaper, talking to some nice architect about gutting the place' (p. 238). For Veronica, justice is achieved through the destruction of the site of Liam's abuse: her anger is directed not towards the deceased perpetrator or her grandmother, Ada, but towards the space. Like the secret itself, the site of the abuse is concealed, hidden away from others.

> I will ask him to get the place cleaned out with something really strong, I don't want a woman with a mop, I will say, I want a team of men in boiler suits with tanks on their backs and those high-pressure steel rods. And the garage – we will turn the garage into a studio space, with skylights and white walls. (p. 238)

Her revenge on the house will begin with chemicals cleaning out the past and any traces of her brother or his abuser. Her revenge is also structural, as she considers ripping 'out the yellow ceiling and the clammy walls, to knock down the doorway to the front room' (p. 238). In removing the through spaces, she is creating an open space subject to interpretation. For her debt or duty to Liam, Veronica has no choice but to interact with the law as the possession of property is a legal process of textual ownership.[54]

The association between the house and mourning is further evident when the body of Liam is returned to his family home. 'Some ancient impulse of my mother's means that she wants the coffin brought back to the house before the removal, so Liam can lie in state in our ghastly front room' (p. 42). Again, the law is inevitably present in the language of mourning and burial as to 'lie in state' is a direct reference to the authoritative doctrine of the governing law. This phrase suggests that the dead body must be on display for members of the public to pay their respects. The return of the body to the state occurs prior to the funeral or removal, as demonstrated by Liam's body dressed: 'in a navy suit with a blue shirt – like a Garda. He would have liked that' (p. 193). As an official representative of the state, Liam's body becomes situated as a guardian, a protector of the law. As a guardian, Liam's body is a protector of thresholds (unlike his ghost) as his body has been determined by the law. As Veronica sees her dead brother for the first time, she is again concerned with the architecture of the house:

> I expected the coffin to be set across the room, but there is not enough space for this. Liam's head points towards the closed curtains and there are candles behind him, set on high stands. I can not see his face properly from where I sit. The wood of the coffin angles down, slicing across the bulge of his cheek. (p. 193)

In the Irish Catholic tradition of burial, the body remains in the house for people to visit, but primarily to be looked at. As Veronica remarks, 'I suppose it is amazing. The viewing moment. When they have left, but are not yet gone. When you are not quite sure what it is you see' (p. 62). Just as Liam's ghost reproduces a threshold by his gaze, the living gaze onto the dead reaffirms the boundary between the living and the dead as the gaze can never be returned. As Julia Kristeva suggests in 'Powers of horror', the corpse must be looked at to demonstrate the state of the living and the dead: 'refuse and corpses *show me* what I permanently thrust aside in order to live . . . there, I am at the border of my condition as a human being.'[55] The act of looking upon a body reaffirms the dividing line between the living and the dead, as the living gaze is simultaneously a lawful one. The gaze of the ghost is as host while the gaze on the body aligns it with a guest. As Foucault writes in *Birth of the Clinic*: 'the gaze is not faithful to truth, nor supreme to it, without asserting, at the same time, a supreme mastery: the gaze that sees is a gaze that dominates.'[56] Hence, the gaze of the living on the dead is the gaze of the master over the slave as the dead body is subject to the governance of the law which will ensure it is banished to the graveyard. As Foucault explores in his epic *Discipline and Punish*, the one who gazes is powerful as there is control and authority through surveillance. Since the law has arrived as guest to oversee Liam's death, the body also becomes a guarding device for the law. In this way, both text and body guard the presence of the law within the house. As Ofrat writes in relation to Kafka's 'Before the law', 'the text as guard and the open-closed gate interdicts entry to the substance of the meaning behind the text'.[57] Due to the insubstantial threshold of the law, the law requires numerous guards, guards that must never face the law. After the initial 'viewing moment', the family retreat into the kitchen rather than sit in with the body, although it is never allowed to remain alone. Veronica's sister 'Kitty is on duty by the far wall in case a mourner should be left indecently alone with the corpse, in case the corpse should be left indecently alone' (p. 193). That the corpse needs to be guarded suggests a vulnerability in death as assurance is required that the body will not be treated disrespectfully. There is also the suggestion that the body should not be left alone; the body is thus surrounded by an absent audience, with Kitty guarding the body that is determined by the law. The legal force that dictates the ritual of mourning ensures that the thresholds within the house are carefully guarded.

Like the mourners assembled for Liam's wake, gatherings are associated with death. After Veronica's father dies, the symbol of the staircase is once again recalled by the mourners: '"He would have been so proud to see you all", one of the neighbours said. "So proud. Sitting in a row, like steps and stairs"' (pp. 42–3). After the death of the patriarch, the mourners again attempt to reconfigure presence in a time of absence. The Hegarty family is comprised of twelve siblings whose existence is determined in relation to the architecture of the home. 'It is possible that we sat, even then, in order of age, "steps and stairs" as people used to croon, although the staircase was now bocketty, with gaps and broken planks and disproportion between one fat stoop and the next' (p. 85). As the years go by and various family members die, the staircase that is symbolic of the family lineage becomes uneven, resulting in a disjointed staircase. Running parallel to one another, the staircase and the chimney act as pathways through the centre of the house that ensure the ability of the house to stand. Comparing the children of the dead patriarch with a staircase suggests a reassurance of lineage and presence, as although the father is dead his legacy is assured.

As children, Veronica, Liam and their sister Kitty are forced to pay their respects to the body of their grandfather, Charlie. To do so, they must climb the stairs to where his body has been laid in his bedroom. This journey of mourning is made evident by the mourners gathered on the staircase. 'The neighbours' feet stuck out a surprising distance from the step where they each knelt: their shoes waggled mid-air' (p. 60). In mourning, the guests produce a second staircase, an additional support for the structure of the house. Heidegger's discourse associates 'the proximity of Being with the values of neighboring, shelter, house, service, guard, voice, and listening'.[58] In death, the security of the home, inheritance and lineage are threatened and therefore the role of the visiting mourner is to support the backbone of the house to keep it standing at all costs. Heidegger's 'identification of the word *logos* as a "gathering" in a way that lets things "stand"'[59] emphasizes the necessity of architectural support during mourning. As Mark Wigley suggests, 'the figure of the edifice, the grounded structure, is that of a standing up that represents'.[60] Traditionally, the supplementary presences on the stairs provide weight and substance to the invasion of absence after the death of a family member. As remarked at Liam's funeral, '"Suicides always pull a good crowd"' (p. 240). The gathering or wake is a cultural practice that deals with death through congregation: as the corpse of Liam is returned to the home to lie in state, the private space becomes public through the uncanny presentation of a corpse, and the status of guest is taken one step further. Liam, like Veronica, once lived in the house, and yet after his death he becomes something other, no longer belonging to the house or people in it, as 'abjection persists as exclusion or taboo'.[61] Liam is excluded from the family and yet his body has taken on the status of guest, welcomed into the house not as a member of the family but a visitor. This contradiction can be understood through Derrida's discussion of the term 'conjuration' in *Specters of Marx*, a term that has a dual meaning: 'on the one hand, [conjuration suggests] the conspiracy of those who promise solemnly, sometimes secretly, by swearing together an oath to struggle against a superior power.'[62] Marx's simultaneous desire to banish the ghost and to conjure it complicates this definition: 'conjuration signifies, *on the other hand*, the magical incantation destined to *evoke*, to bring forth with the voice, to *convoke* a charm or a spirit.'[63] Hence, the body of Liam is simultaneously welcomed and banished into the front room away from the mourners who gather in the kitchen. In this way, mourners expel that which they have gazed upon, assisting the abjection process of casting the body out of the house. Ironically, the hospitable welcoming of mourners becomes a celebration of eviction. Like evicting someone from a house, the eventual removal of the body will ensure that 'to exclude is to include . . . Expulsion is consumption. To lock something up doesn't involve simply imprisoning it within four walls. It is imprisoned simply by being banned.'[64] Just as the law purports to exclude and include, all subjects of the law are inevitably bound within it. Hence, gathering to expel becomes a lawful charge, an accumulation of mourners that attempt to reassure (through exclusion) that the dead remain within the appropriate realm. And yet, through the absent presence of the ghost, expulsion (like mourning) is shown to be impossible.

Before the body is introduced into the home, it must be domesticated. As discussed by Mark Wigley, philosophy has domesticated the house through language as an 'exemplar of representation' or 'paradigm of place' as 'to dominate is always to house, to place in the *domus*. Domination is domestication.'[65] By taming that which has the potential to be other, philosophy governs the space. The same is true for Liam's body as before he is welcomed into the house he must be deemed acceptable to enter. Instead of appearing other, Liam must be dressed in a suit and made to look as normal as possible. After observing Liam's body, Veronica's husband remarks that '"he looks like an estate agent"' (p. 199). Rather than reveal how the law of hospitality has permitted the monstrous, the absurd has been permitted instead. Estate agents, however, are stereotypically described as parasites that live off the surplus from selling houses. As Derrida writes in *Limited Inc*: 'Parasitism takes place when the parasite comes to live *off the life* of the body in which it resides – and when reciprocally, the host incorporates the parasite to an extent, willy nilly offering it hospitality: providing it with a place.'[66] Liam's appearance reinforces his status as guest, as estate agents hold several keys to several houses, and yet live in none of them. The role of agent in this context is to visit whilst remaining parasitical, or supplementary to the site.

The tradition of the wake insists that mourners gaze upon the dead while feasting: mourners are encouraged to gorge themselves with food, to fill their stomachs with substance. Veronica remarks that 'we eat it all up. Down to the apple tart and ice cream. We do not stint. We put slabs of butter on bad white rolls, and we ask for second cups of tea. I am inordinately interested in the food' (p. 247). The visiting guests and mourners are attempting to fill the absence left behind by the dead. While the body is in the front room, simultaneously occupying and not occupying space, the guests are uncannily engaged with food. The guests become obsessed with gorging themselves as a fundamental element of hospitality is the offering of food. Through this example of hospitality, the borders of the house are aligned with digestion.

> Buildings are bound to consumption. For philosophy, there is a struc-
> tural affinity between architecture, physical desire, eating and drinking
> ... there should be no consumption in the ideal house, no exchange
> within or across its borders ... The figure of the house is that of
> exclusion that maintains a line between inside and outside, while the
> digestive system is that which confuses inside and outside, endlessly
> folding the limit, transforming one into the other.[67]

The potential of the house to digest represents an immense vulnerability of the borders that constitute it. Instead of a secure architectural
standing that contains those within, the thresholds of the house can
be understood as coinciding folds. As guests enter to consume the
inside of the home, hospitality permits exchange. Just as the body
of Liam is permitted entry, the house must expel him through an act
of digestion, an act that disturbs the boundaries of the home rather
than securing them. Once the body is admitted, thresholds remain
persistently disturbed as the attempt to expel and maintain those
boundaries permanently alters them. As suggested in the introduction
to this book, once boundaries have been disturbed, they cannot be
reinstated. Furthermore, as the narrative suggestively advocates, 'there
will be another 10 days at least to wait before they can feast on Liam's
poor corpse, because of the paperwork involved' (p. 10). Therefore,
the feasting associated with mourning can be read as a feeding on
the corpse itself. Symbolically, the consumption of food is actually
the gorging of the corpse. Hence, the mourners metaphorically
assist the expulsion by digesting the body in order to expel it through
the emission of excrement.

As the 10 days of waiting suggest, Veronica's work of mourning
begins with waiting for the arrival of her brother's body. As Goodrich
suggests, 'for Freud, the "work" of mourning is that of the subject's
coming to terms with the reality of loss'.[68] Such a process is depicted
as being one of 'intense struggle through which the mourner slowly
parts with a continued existence, the internal image or hallucination
through which the lost object lives on in the mind of the mourner'.[69]
Due to the impossibility of mourning, Veronica places Liam in an
internal crypt in a moment of simultaneous exclusion and inclusion.
Contrary to the traditional belief of burying the dead to rest in
peace, the dead remain with the living, resulting in a mourning

that is not a process of expulsion. As Derrida writes in *Ear of the Other*,

> Not having been taken back inside the self, digested, assimilated as in all 'normal' mourning, the dead object remains like a living dead abscessed in a specific spot in the ego. It has its place, just like a crypt in a cemetery or temple, surrounded by walls and all the rest. The dead object is incorporated in this crypt – the term 'incorporated' signalling precisely that one has failed to digest or assimilate totally, so that it remains there, forming a pocket in the mourning body . . . I fail to do what Freud calls the normal work of mourning, with the result that the dead person continues to inhabit me, but as a stranger. By contrast, in normal mourning, if such a thing exists, I take the dead upon myself, I digest it, assimilate it, idealise it.[70]

Instead of 'digesting' her dead brother, Veronica 'houses' him in a mental vault, a space that corrupts the mourning process and abjects Liam as 'a stranger', and therefore removes his otherness. As a form of parasite, Liam becomes 'a foreign body within one's own body, taken into the body precisely to stop it from contaminating and disfiguring the body by keeping it withdrawn in indefinite quarantine'.[71] Like the indigestible secret, she carries him as baggage or a foreign weight that has become a host inhabiting her mind. In this way, mourning is aligned with the indigestion of the ghost: that which cannot be exchanged remains. 'A house, then, is no more than the repression of a constitutional indigestion',[72] attempting to domesticate the fear of permitting entry to the uninvited. As the law of the household is intricately aligned with the law itself, mourning 'internalises loss, marks a certain desire, it marks the limit threshold and, in a sense, the failure of law'.[73] In attempting to distance the living from the memory of the dead, mourning becomes a ritual heavily reliant upon spatial metaphor, a ritual that also highlights the limit of the law's involvement in death. Because of her brother's ghost, Veronica cannot mourn effectively as the effects of his gaze persist. As a foreign body, however, Liam is preserved in her mind as a stranger, an uncanny presence that haunts. Like Max in chapter 3, she does not digest the other through mourning, but preserves both Liam's memory and the unspeakable secret associated with him. In Veronica's case, she

---

preserves the guilt she experienced after refusing to reveal the horrific secret of Liam's abuse. Therefore, her refusal to mourn is bound to her sense of duty, a duty that she failed to demonstrate towards the demands of her brother's ghost.[74]

Her impossible mourning suggests that Veronica did not follow the predetermined pathway of mourning, as such a ritual ensures the dead 'are kept in their place'. As she observes in England, 'there is a line on the landscape that refuses to move, it slides backwards instead, and that is where I fix my eye' (p. 44). Instead of a linear progression, she decides to remain in the past, forever providing hospitality to the guilt that has become the memory of her deceased brother. In this way, she perverts an already perverted law, as the most hospitable realm is the vault within her, 'both the hiding of a secret and the hiding of that hiding'.[75] After unbuilding all architectural spaces around her, her most successful building is achieved through failed mourning, the building of a crypt within herself, a hospitality that will refuse only one guest: the law.

5

An Inherited Poison: Hamlet, The Castle of Otranto *and* Lunar Park

ی

With the publication of *Lunar Park*, Bret Easton Ellis established himself as a contributor to the newly emergent field of postmodern horror. Through an interrogation of authoritative structures, this chapter will demonstrate how Ellis's novel presents a time that is 'out of joint',[1] figuring a dislocation that makes the notion of father-son inheritance impossible. Ellis's postmodernity is immediately suggested by an ambiguous authorial voice, as his protagonist, Bret Easton Ellis, shares not only his name, but also his infamous past and familial history. Through the positioning of authorial self as fictional protagonist, Ellis enters into a complex self-conscious game, opening his text up to multiple interpretations even though the inscription of the authorial voice seems to furnish it with a closed and definitive meaning. As Jacques Derrida famously put it in relation to the autobiographical inscriptions of Jean-Jacques Rousseau, 'there is nothing outside of the text'.[2] For far from facilitating the transparent transmissions of the author, it is language itself, in Derrida's view, that begins to speak, with secrecy and textuality within language becoming the order of the day. And as this chapter will argue, it is precisely the ability of language to transmit a clear and authoritative message that ultimately becomes one of the main preoccupations in *Lunar Park*. As the Gothic is concerned with improper inheritances, Ellis's allusion to the Gothic questions an institution reliant on linearity. Thus, flaws within the traditional system of inheritance are apparent, reducing lineage to an impossible model subject to multiple errors. As Derrida suggests in *For what Tomorrow*, 'the best way to be faithful to a heritage is to be unfaithful, that is, not to accept it literally, as a totality'.[3] Perversely, horror becomes the most faithful response to a tradition that exceeds its own boundaries. Through examination of a tradition, one can develop an alternative understanding of the complex forces that permit that system to function. The system is both perverted and reinforced by this alternative knowledge.

Like Kurtz's experience of the heart of darkness in Joseph Conrad's novel of that name, Bret's horror is 'the horror' of those very words: the dissemination of signification suggested through the innumerable associations between signifiers.[4] Here, horror is initiated through a dissemination of meaning, an uncertainty that shakes the foundations of authoritative structures such as history, patriarchy and the law. Just as Kurtz cannot articulate his dark journey through the Congo, so Bret's horror challenges the language of linearity and traditional understandings of inheritance. Through the return of his father's ghost, Bret witnesses a usurpation of linearity that, ironically, attempts to reaffirm the authoritative role of the father. As Derrida has argued in *Specters of Marx*, the authority of the spectral father is undermined through his apparition, a dislocation that makes inheritance impossible. For Derrida, the tradition of Western metaphysics is haunted by traces of what it has attempted to disparage and discard, resulting in repeated instances of times and beings that are variously 'out of joint'. Through *différance*, traces of unintended meaning are aligned with each signifier, reducing the accuracy of just such a system in the process. The threat to the system is contained within that system, a tradition held together by these contradictory forces. Through an inheritance that is poisonous in its effects, *Lunar Park* interrogates an irresponsible father whose authority over his son results in fatal consequences. Hence the law of the father is undermined by his own actions as the threat to the system is not reassuringly outside, but, like Poe's 'Red Death', disturbingly within.

Lunar Park is haunted by the classic themes of Shakespeare's *Hamlet*. In *Specters of Marx*, Derrida argues that Hamlet 'curses the destiny that would precisely have destined him, to do justice, to put things back in order, so that, in conformity with the rule of its correct functioning, it advances straight ahead – and following the law'.[5]

The securing of legacy is achieved only through the linear structure of the unbroken line, the bloodline that passes from generation to generation. The appearance of the spectre, however, disrupts this configuration of legacy by punctuating the smooth line of inheritance with irregularities. In reclaiming his last wishes, the spectre of the father both obeys and defies the rules of legacy. The rights of the father are asserted, but through his return, lineage has also been disrupted. As Bret remarks, 'I kept picturing a gray river made of ash flowing backwards'.[6] This suggests a reversed lineage, a disturbed pathway, as the father has returned after death to disrupt the very linearity of inheritance that he attempts to secure. This attempt to secure and re-establish lineage results in a horror that destroys from within: the apparition of the father dislocates the correct sequence of events, suggesting an alternative, impossible experience of inheritance.

In *Lunar Park*, Bret is addressed by the spectre of the father that appears after he has ignored the wishes outlined in his last will and testament. As such, Bret is a Hamlet-like figure who (initially) does not 'sweare' to carry out his father's wishes after death. As Derrida suggests, 'the father's death opens a reign of violence'.[7] Indeed, the spirit of the father horrifies Bret and – like Hamlet – causes him to act manically and unlawfully. As Bret observes: 'I had the dehydrated and haggard face of a man ten years older, and my eyes were so red that you couldn't see the irises.'[8] Through the horror of an impossible lineage, the son also becomes aesthetically hideous, with defining aspects of his identity such as age distorted. Like any Gothic monster, his eyes become red, indicating the poisonous effects he has inherited from a spectral father. Upon returning to his childhood home, Bret remarks that 'my sisters marvelled at how much I had begun resembling our father as I moved toward middle age' (p. 410). In a moment of uncanny replication, Bret exhibits his father's characteristics, symptomatic of an inherited noxious bloodline. This haunting suggests that the parasite that provokes the downfall of a tradition comes from within; the threat is not from outside, but contained in the structure itself and integral to its functioning. Ellis thus highlights poisonous parental relationships, the haunting effects of which can only result in chaos. Instead of the customary importance of the father's word, *Lunar Park* represents the destructive abilities of the father-son relationship.

In its debt to *Hamlet*, *Lunar Park* opens with a quotation from the play: 'From the table of my memory/I'll wipe away all trivial fond records/All saws of books, all forms, all pressures past/That youth and observation copied there.'[9] This quotation highlights the complex relationship between *Lunar Park* and the patriarchal literary tradition. By invoking the act of erasure, Ellis alludes to a rejection of knowledge and learning while asserting the apparent insignificance of an inherited canonical tradition. Taken in its original moment, the quotation refers to Hamlet's replacement of his prior sense of knowledge with the horror of his father's demands. In this simultaneous act of erasure and inscription, the ghost of his father has usurped Hamlet's mind, rewriting his thoughts as if the mind were a surface for inscription. Like a palimpsest, or Freud's 'mystic writing pad', Bret's memory is subject to an interchange of erasure and inscription. As Ophelia remarks, 'O, what a noble mind is here o'erthrown!'[10] Like the supernatural that exceeds the boundary of the natural, Hamlet's mind is exceeded and rewritten by the poison inherited from his father. The ability of the ghost to overthrow the mind of the son suggests the autonomy of the spectral, as power is aligned not with tradition but rather its ruin. Although Hamlet's father is, in a sense, the legitimate ruler, his death renders him illegitimate, and yet he still exercises power. It is thus through acts of haunting in Shakespeare that power structures are annulled. In turn, a concern with correcting lines of inheritance and the unlawful usurpation of power repeatedly haunts the Gothic. Through employment of the spectral, the Gothic usurps tradition itself, rendering all efforts to overcome the horror of a dislocated linearity hopeless. Although Gothic texts offer some sense of resolution, the veiled conclusion is that once systems of meaning such as the authority of the father's word have been tested, they cannot be reinstated: the poison remains forever an integral part of the very structure it attempts to dislocate.

As the first 'Gothic Story', *The Castle of Otranto* presents a time 'out of joint' through the succession of an illegitimate heir, a ruler whose word is (illegally) representative of authority. As is the case with other Gothic texts, Walpole plagiarizes elements from *Hamlet* for his, admitting in his second preface that the 'great master of nature, Shakespeare, was the model I copied'.[11] Although a sense of resolution seems to be achieved at the end of the text, the time 'out of joint' is not set right. Although Theodore, 'the true heir of Alfonso',[12] assumes the principality of Otranto, events are not corrected by the return of the spectral. Instead, they induce a cyclical repetition of events as Theodore is forced to marry Isabella in order to unite family estates. After the death of his true love Matilda, Theodore was 'persuaded he could know no happiness but in the society of one with whom he could forever indulge the melancholy that had taken possession of his soul'.[13] The price of legitimacy is the happiness of the heir. Theodore and Isabella are also related to one another (Isabella's father has a claim to the throne of Otranto), a poor foundation for a marriage that contributed to Manfred's loss of the estate. Therefore, the incestuous foundations for a principality are repeated. Furthermore, the correction of the time 'out of joint' is instigated by the bloody deaths of Manfred's offspring Matilda and Conrad, and the spectres of Manfred's grandfather Ricardo and his betrayed previous employer Alfonso. Therefore, the linearity of inheritance is disrupted by the supernatural and the illegal. Although Ricardo has murdered Alfonso and usurped his role as ruler of Otranto, he is not punished. Instead, his grandson Manfred and great-grandchildren Matilda and Conrad must pay the price for his actions.

Unlike Bret, Hamlet is a son in deep mourning, inhabiting the castle in black, absorbed in his books. Hamlet's uncle who has usurped the throne from Hamlet's father reminds him that 'you must know your father lost a father;/That father lost, lost his, and the survivor bound/In filial obligation for some term/To do obsequious sorrow',[14] and that the time for mourning is therefore at an end. Through a chain of loss, the necessity of lineage and inheritance is apparent. He also suggests that there is a debt to be paid to the lost father as well as to each of the deceased, as each son must mourn for a certain period of time. However, Hamlet insists that he cannot bring the practice of mourning to an (untimely) end. Hamlet remarks that 'The time is out of joint/O cursed spite that ever I was born to set it right!'[15] The linearity of inheritance has been curved (events are not as they should be) and due to the appearance of the ghost, the son must attempt to correct those events. Because of the poison within, events are incomprehensible, resulting in an alternative, impossible experience of inheritance. As Anne Williams writes, 'Hamlet is a young man trying to become himself by coming to terms with his family's past'.[16]

Because of the sins of the father, Hamlet struggles to correlate his own being and sense of responsibility with his ancestry. Like Hamlet, Manfred in *The Castle of Otranto* is responsible for the actions of his grandfather who poisoned his employer Alfonso and usurped the principality of Otranto. As he states: 'he lost no Conrad, no Matilda! I pay the price of usurpation for all!'[17] As inheritor of a poisonous lineage, Manfred is torn between his sense of duty and the morality of his behaviour.

For Hamlet, the death of the father initially brings relief, but through haunting a greater horror develops. As Hamlet puts it, Claudius 'killed my King, and whored my mother/Popped in between th'election and my hopes/[and has] Thrown out his angle for my proper life'.[18] The time 'out of joint' has resulted in the improper and the immoral as events occur outside the law. Through the apparition of the father, the horror weighs upon the son, and yet the son cannot right such a perversion. As a revenge play, *Hamlet* does not lawfully restore that which has been usurped. Instead, Hamlet, prompted by his father, must take the law into his own hands. As Derrida's reading suggests, the son, 'in order to make up for the father's death, transgressed the law. He repeated the father's death. These two gestures contradict each other or cancel each other out.'[19] Like the *pharmakon*, the lawful word of the father is illegal, a conflation of oppositional terms in the same act. The moral implications of this are extreme, as the spectre induces a sense of lawlessness in the son and actions that will result in chaos. Such illegality is introduced through the very apparition of the spectre: 'bringing the ghost back in a temporally disjunctive manner destabilise[s] the cognition of temporal order as a perceived sequence of events. The spectral is, therefore, a matter of recognising what is disorderly within an apparently straightforward temporal framework.'[20] Through the father's return, the son is forced into illegality and immorality as he becomes an unlawful subject outside of the limits of the law. With Bret an outlaw, the father dislocates the linearity of inheritance, as through the spectre's challenge of authority and tradition the father's dynasty is annulled. Like his horrific appearance, Bret becomes suggestive of an inherited horror that, like the *pharmakon*, is both cure and poison.[21] The father's actions attempt to secure (or cure) a legacy that is dislocated further by that very attempt. Therefore, the impossible event of inheritance is determined by its simultaneous succession and failure. As seen so regularly in Gothic fiction, the succession of the legitimate heir arrives alongside the disruption induced by the spectral. As the *pharmakon* suggests, several meanings are carried by a signifier which can lead the reader astray into a time and language that is 'out of joint'.

Through the combined effects of a dislocated temporality and the illegal demands of a spectre, inheritance becomes imbued with poisonous effects: this is a father who does not always act responsibly or according to the law. This is signified through the recurrent reference to poison in *Hamlet*. As the ghost explains: 'thy uncle stole/With juice of cursed hebona in a vial/And in the porches of my ears did pour/The leperous distilment, whose effect/Holds such an enmity with blood of man.'[22] The usurpation of Old Hamlet is achieved through poison, a lethal liquid that is reminiscent of the bloodline that Hamlet will inherit. Just as his father has been poisoned, so too is the son. The illegal events of the father's death infect the son like a virus, 'like the bite of a poisonous snake [inducing] philosophic *mania*'.[23] Through the impossible knowledge of the father's death, mania is induced in the son: an infection not from outside, but from a dormant poison within. This is further suggested by Claudius as brother and murderer, as the poison that kills Old Hamlet is his own blood (relative). As Claudius pours the liquid into his brother's ears, so the destructive abilities of the *pharmakon* are aligned with the organ of hearing: perversely, Claudius forces his brother to hear his own death from his hands.

As retribution, Hamlet inherits his uncle's methods and disseminates the poisoned bloodline within. As with the *pharmakon*, his own source of life is both cure and poison: cure to the injustice of his father's death, but also poisonous in so far as it results in his own death. Although he escapes the poisoned cup of wine provided by his uncle, Hamlet is slain by a 'poisoned and unbated rapier' wielded by Laertes. As his killer observes, 'no medicine in the world can do thee good':[24] there is no remedy or cure for the inherited virulent blood that has resulted in Hamlet's young and untimely death. The same poisoned rapier causes the deaths of Laertes and Claudius. As Laertes suggests, 'the foul practice hath turned itself on me'[25] as a weapon of defence has become the very source of his demise. This ambivalence is further emphasized by the accidental poisoning of Hamlet's mother, 'the drink, the drink – O my dear Hamlet – /The drink, the drink! I am poisoned!'[26] Although Claudius did not intend to kill his wife, her ingestion of the poison suggests the dissemination of a virulent bloodline through the seemingly beneficial effects of the wine. As Claudius tries to encourage Hamlet to drink the poisoned wine, he cries, 'Here's to thy health!'[27] The wine is aligned with medicinal benefits, yet it is in fact the absolute opposite. After Claudius escapes death by poison, Hamlet repeatedly stabs him with the poisoned dagger while commanding: 'venom to thy work!'[28] Similarly, it is an inherited poison that destroys Bret: 'My father had blackened my perception of the world, and his sneering, sarcastic attitude toward everything had latched onto me. As much as I wanted to escape his influence, I couldn't. It had soaked into me' (p. 8). *Lunar Park* inherits an inescapable venomous lineage that induces a chaotic sequence of events as the validity of the father's word is thrown into doubt.

Like blood, 'sperm, water, ink, paint, perfumed dye: the *pharmakon* always penetrates like a liquid . . . In liquid, opposites are more easily mixed . . . And water, pure liquidity, is most easily and dangerously penetrated then corrupted by the *pharmakon*.'[29] As a liquid, blood (like sperm) suggests dissemination and multiplicity, an openness to corruption. The dissemination associated with fatherhood is apparent in *Otranto* when both Theodore and Isabella are introduced to their fathers for the first time. As the Gothic has always been preoccupied with filial relationships, their union is (initially) romanticized. However, as in *Hamlet* and *Lunar Park*, relationships with the father are presented as deeply problematic. Theodore and Isabella have grown up without a father, and even when they are confronted with their relative they do not know him. Unlike mothers who are traditionally easy to locate, there are multiple possibilities for fathers. When Jerome claims Theodore as his own, Manfred asks: '"How can he be thy son?"'[30] Jerome replies: '"Dost thou question his being mine?"' (p. 57) Such questioning suggests that paternity is not securely located. As Theodore himself says: '"If I am this venerable man's son . . ."' (p. 57); the son's use of the term 'if' posits fatherhood as a possibility, as like the disseminative qualities of sperm, fatherhood is deferred and unlocatable. This multiplicity contradicts the authority of a linear system such as inheritance. With multiple possibilities and offspring not able to recognize their fathers, the dominance of the father's word is both fragile and non-specific. Therefore, as Manfred states, inheritance requires 'numerous supports' (p. 24).

Isabella's father is wearing armour as a disguise when she meets him for the very first time: 'Hippolita demanded of Frederic the cause of his having taken that mysterious course for reclaiming his daughter' (p. 80). By wearing the armour, he asserts an authority of disclosure, choosing to reveal both his identity and his relation to Isabella when he pleases. After he removes the armour, Isabella is unaware that Frederic is her father: 'the stranger, opening his eyes, and beholding a woman, said, Art thou – pray tell me truly – art thou Isabella of Viczena? I am, said she; good heaven restore thee! – Then thou – then thou – said the knight, struggling for utterance – seest – thy father!' (p. 79). Although Frederic has been (mistakenly) injured by Theodore, his struggle to articulate the declaration of fatherhood further suggests his authority of disclosure. Due to his injuries, Isabella is forced to return to the castle to ensure his welfare: 'she followed mournfully behind' (p. 79). Therefore, gaining a father automatically binds her to an unspoken responsibility that determines her submission to the will of Manfred. Instead of protecting his daughter and assisting her flight from Manfred, Frederic supports his plan to marry Isabella. Due to Frederic's own desire for Manfred's daughter Matilda, the two men sacrifice their own offspring to satisfy their own selfish desires. Manfred 'proposed the double marriage. That weak prince, who had been struck with the charms of Matilda, listened but too eagerly to the offer . . . he looked upon his own succession to the principality as facilitated by wedding Matilda' (p. 96). Although she has only just met her father, Isabella is convinced of his integrity: '"my father is too pious, too noble", interrupted Isabella, "to command an impious deed. But should he command it, can a father enjoin a cursed act?"' (p. 91). Although expectations of her father's morality are high, Isabella quickly becomes aware of the unspoken duty a child has to her parents. Ultimately, both fathers found in *Otranto* have a poisonous effect on their recently claimed offspring.

When Theodore meets his father, Father Jerome, he has no indication that the religious man is the long-lost father he has been seeking. As he is in the process of removing his shirt to be executed by Manfred, his parentage is revealed by 'the mark of a bloody arrow. Gracious heaven! cried the holy man starting, what do I see? It is my child! my Theodore!' (p. 57). This bloody stain is suggestive of the poisonous lineage he has inherited, from a man whose fall from Count to 'holy man' left his wife and son destitute. The trauma associated with the duty of lineage is indicated through Theodore's precarious position: his father is introduced just as he is about to be slain. Although Jerome attempts to save his son's life when he realizes who he is, the religious man readily admits that it is his interference that has brought about his son's demise. As he ignited Manfred's jealousy of Theodore by suggesting Isabella's affection for him, Jerome tells his son "'I am thy murderer! It is I have brought this dismal hour upon thee!'" (p. 56). Because of Jerome's intervention, Manfred nearly decapitates Theodore. Like Isabella, Theodore quickly accepts the dominance of familial duty to which he is now subject: 'Theodore, like Isabella, was too recently acquainted with parental authority' (p. 93). As Jerome realizes Theodore's affections for Manfred's daughter, he 'was heartily grieved to discover his son's inclination for that princess' (p. 93) and incites the vengeance of his own ancestors to induce a change of heart: 'kneel, headstrong boy, and list, while a father unfolds a tale of horror, that will expel every sentiment from thy soul, but sensations of sacred vengeance' (p. 94). Acquiring a father instigates a duty to an unquestionable authority, a lineage that initiates a poisonous effect on the offspring. Although Theodore claims to love Matilda, he is subject to his father's judgement: "'but could I gaze on thee, and remember thou art sprung from the tyrant Manfred?'" (p. 73).

In *Lunar Park*, the ghost of the father suggests a spectral patriarchy that is dismissed by the son when he ignores his will. His father's return, however, signifies a (subversive) correction of events, a removal of power from the son who has ignored the father's last words. As Derrida remarks in *Specters of Marx*: 'The one who says "I am thy Father's Spirit" can only be taken at his word.'[31] The word of the father is a command, but it is also the law. After his father's death, Bret states that

His ashes were put into a bag – even though his (invalid) will stated that he wanted his children to spread them at sea off the coast of Cabo San Lucas, where he vacationed frequently – we stored the ashes in a safe-deposit box in a Bank of America on Ventura Boulevard next to a dilapidated McDonalds. (p. 21)

Bret's description of the ashes locates them very precisely. For Derrida, mourning 'consists always in attempting to ontologise remains, to make them present, in the first place by *identifying* the bodily remains and by *localizing* the dead'.[32] By locating the ashes so specifically, Bret exercises power over the patriarch by denouncing his will as 'invalid'. The ability to interpret the textual permits a redistribution of power that temporarily allows the son to go against his father's wishes. Perversely, his dismissal of the father's demands betrays a heritage even while remaining faithful to it: ignoring the father's word would ironically result in order for the son. As a reminding remainder of his father's poisonous influence, Bret ensures his ashes are outside the home.

After his father's death, Bret becomes the head of his family: 'my father made me trustee of his estate' (p. 21). However, as slave to his father's illegal demands, he inherits nothing. His father's legacy is worthless, as the aftermath of his father's death is a 'protracted legal battle with the IRS' (p. 21). Although Bret inherits his father's estate, his legacy is without value, as his father 'owed millions in back taxes' (p. 21). Bret's inheritance is an accumulation of status rather than capital; the Hamlet of this text inherits a loss as he gains his father's debts to pay. Instead of simply gaining nothing, Bret inherits a negative value, an impossibility that cannot be articulated through traditional understandings of inheritance which insist on gain. Through such an incomprehensible event, inheritance is declared impossible. This is further evident when Bret discloses the fact that his father 'made the bulk of his money from highly speculative real estate deals' (p. 7). The estate that Bret inherits has been generated by the exchange of property, a practice intimately connected with the law. Such exchange, however, is achieved through 'highly speculative' illegal deals for increased profit, making his father an outlaw. After his father's death, Bret is burdened with heavy debts just as he has inherited a poisonous lineage. Even before he encounters his father's ghost, the horror of inheritance is evident.

His attainment of loss extends much further than financial issues, as Bret also inherits the indignity of his father's death, a death that he again attempts to localize specifically: 'he was found naked by the twenty-two-year-old girlfriend on the bathroom floor of his empty house in Newport Beach' (p. 20). In death, his father was humiliated, and as his son, Bret is humiliated too. Bret inherits the disgrace of the father in the last moments of his life, including by way of his possessions, 'two Patek Philippe watches and a boxful of oversized Armani suits' (p. 21). Bret is horrified to discover that 'the inseams in the crotch of the trousers were stained with blood, which we later found out was the result of a botched penile implant' (pp. 21–2). In an uncanny act of inheritance, Bret holds his father's blood in his hands, a sign of the poisonous bloodline passed from father to son. Just as the ash induces horror, so his father's blood stains the inherited garment as poison has stained Bret's existence. 'My father, in his last years, due to the toxic mix of diabetes and alcoholism, had become impotent' (p. 22). The blood in the Armani suits also represents the fallen father in his inability to reproduce, his body scarred by an attempted addition to his body induced by fears of an insecure lineage. The irregularities of his father's corpse before cremation indicate the punctuated process of inheritance in *Lunar Park*, a monstrous body reminiscent of the horror that inheritance will instigate. Though the father has disgraced the son, the son has also dishonoured the father in his last moments as 'the coroner was mystified by certain irregularities. No one wanted to pursue these irregularities and he was cremated immediately' (p. 21). Through the poisonous line of inheritance, the son is bound to act like the father. In life, as in death, they are caught up in a dynamic of mutual betrayal. Bret betrays his role as son by dismissing the 'irregularities' of his father's body, while the father betrays his patriarchal role by corrupting his son's behaviour. The irregularities in his autopsy suggest a lack (or proliferation) of meaning, an uncategorizable death that, in all respects, resists closure. Instead of acting on these irregularities, Bret chooses to ignore them until haunting forces him to reconsider the father. As Derrida suggests, 'an heir is not only someone who receives, he or she is someone who chooses, and who takes the risk of deciding'.[33] Like Hamlet, Bret initially hesitates over his role as heir. As Hamlet muses, 'to be or not to be – that is the question,/Whether 'tis nobler in the mind to suffer/The slings and arrows of outrageous fortune/Or to take arms against a sea of troubles'.[34] Such is the role of inheritor that Bret and Hamlet must eventually submit to the law of the father, and, as such, there is no real or meaningful choice available. As Derrida suggests, 'the seed must thus submit to *logos*. And in so doing, it must do violence to itself, since the natural tendency of sperm is opposed to the law of *logos*.'[35] Due to the dissemination of sperm that tradition-ally ensures inheritance, the seed (or the son) aligns itself with the multiplicity of meanings and possibilities within language. However, the son must submit to the law of the father, and in doing so, he commits violence against himself. Through its preoccupations with father-son relationships, *Lunar Park* repeatedly suggests a simultaneous act of remedying and poisoning lineage, just as the *pharmakon* can be 'alternately or simultaneously – beneficent or maleficent'.[36]

Just as Old Hamlet's ghost appears on the battlements of the castle at Elsinore, so the apparition of Bret's father occurs in the centre of his house. As the home is symbolic of an ownership that will be inherited by the next generation, the site of the home has become infected by the poisonous influence of the father. Bret describes how

> The living room might as well have been a screen and the house a theatre. It [the ghost] was lurching down the staircase, pausing on various steps. It was tall and had a vaguely human form, and though it was skeletal it had eyes. (p. 401)

Like Hamlet, the horrific gaze of his father's ghost causes Bret to act, to right the wrong that he has committed. Although he knows it to be his father, Bret insists upon the word 'it' to describe the spectre, a clear admission that the apparition defies conventional categor-ization. The lack of a proper body is emphasized by the presence of eyes; through his vision, the father can exercise judgement over the son. The father appears to the son by descending down the stairs in a metaphorical removal of patriarchal power. A few chapters later, Bret is attacked on the staircase, resulting in a scarring lameness. His attempt to climb the stairs and reach the top is disrupted by the wounds in his leg. His attempt to ascend the patriarchal hierarchy (represented by a house or an estate) is interrupted, as the steps became 'slippery from all the blood pouring from the wound in my thigh' (p. 429). Like his father at the moment of his death, Bret has become weak and lame with the stain of poisoned blood on his clothes. The spilling of his blood on the staircase creates a vertical bloodline, the stain of inheritance in the space of the house. This trail of blood extends through the house, marking it with the blood of inheritance: 'beyond my trail of blood the door was bulging forward' (p. 432). This is reiterated when Bret realizes that the face of the ghost keeps changing: 'it was the face of a father being replaced by the face of a son' (p. 402). Such an interchange highlights how the son and father are locked in a poisonous ritual, a dialogue that threatens to engulf them both. As Horatio remarks to Hamlet on the apparition of his father, 'The very place puts toys of desperation/Without more motive, into every brain'.[37] Through the appearance of the father, the son becomes a desperate man, an outlaw suggestive of the poisonous bloodline. After his father's reappearance, Hamlet kills Laertes's father, Polonius. The multiple transgressions induced by the father suggest an unlawful influence rather than an authoritatively moral and legal power.

Unlike Theodore and Isabella, Matilda and Conrad retain a father figure throughout *The Castle of Otranto*. The results of this are extremely negative: both characters are killed either directly (in Matilda's case) or indirectly (Conrad) by their father Manfred. Sickly Conrad is buried by the weight of lineage through a gigantic, supernatural helmet and Matilda is (mistakenly) murdered by her father with a dagger: '"heaven directed my bloody hand to the heart of my child!"'[38] The reason for their deaths is the unlawful usurpation of Otranto, an event that occurred three generations before they were born. As the rightful heir, Alfonso, 'died by poison' (p. 113) administered by Manfred's grandfather Ricardo, Manfred's lineage is based on a falsified will. This illegal usurpation is inherited by his progeny, a poison symbolic of the act of inheritance. As Manfred admits, '"ye would say he came not fairly to his end – It is most true – why else this bitter cup which Manfred must drink to the dregs?"' (p. 113). Like the initial poison administered to Alfonso, Manfred must also consume the medicinal effects of a corrupt lineage. After he is confronted with the ghost of his grandfather, he exclaims: '"speak infernal spectre! Or, if thou art my grandsire, why dost thou too conspire against thy wretched descendant, who too dearly pays for–"' (p. 26). Manfred halts his sentence before he declares the unspeakable horror he has incurred through his lineage.

Due to the prophecy that the principality will remain in his family as long as there are sons to maintain it, Manfred becomes manic in his quest for a son. 'Reasons of state, most urgent reasons, my own and the safety of my people, demand that I should have a son' (p. 49). The pressure to produce a male heir, a duty that has been inherited from the ancestral event of murder, induces a state of madness and paranoia. 'Manfred, walking as from a trance, beat his breast, [and] twisted his hands in his locks' (p. 109). As a man dealing with a turbulent filial history, Manfred is, like Hamlet and Bret, torn between his duty to lineage and the moral consequences of his actions. 'He dashed himself on the ground, and cursed the day he was born' (p. 110). He is not, however, purely tyrannical. Instead, he shows regret for actions that are not his at all: 'Manfred was not one of those savage tyrants who wanton in cruelty unprovoked. The circumstances of his fortune had given an asperity to his temper, which was naturally humane' (p. 33). Due to the illegal events that determined his role as Prince of Otranto, Manfred's character adapts, forcing him to act in ways that he is not proud of, as he was 'ashamed too of his inhuman treatment of a princess, who returned every injury with new marks of tenderness and duty' (p. 38). Like the simultaneously medicinal and poisonous qualities of the *pharmakon*, Manfred requires a son to cure his anxious lineage, and yet this can only be achieved by acting illegally. In turn, this behaviour ultimately results in the demise of his family line with the loss of their claim to the principality of Otranto. Therefore, the cure to maintain his lineage is also the poison that will usurp his inherited title.

Manfred's frustrations are further aggravated by his wife, Hippolita. His 'reflections on her sterility, who had given him but one heir' (p. 17), can be attributed to their ancestry: as Manfred declares to Jerome, '"we are related within the forbidden degrees"' (p. 69). The horror of incest is such that the illegalities of the parentage are revisited upon the kin, as suggested by Conrad's ill health and Matilda's doomed fate. As Manfred states '"too long has she cursed me by her unfruitfulness. My fate depends on having sons"' (p. 25). Manfred's son, however, is 'a homely youth, sickly, and of no promising disposition' (p. 17). His weak constitution can be attributed to the incestuous relations of his parents, indicating further the simultaneous benefits and detriments of the *pharmakon*. Because of the obsession with maintaining the family's claim over Otranto, Manfred and Hippolita are married to ensure the continuity of the lineage. However, as evidenced by ancient royal families, incest often results in unhealthy offspring. The perpetuation of lineage (incest) is also its poison.

Similarly, Manfred's urgency for Conrad to be married, 'that he might celebrate the wedding as soon as Conrad's infirm state of health would permit' (p. 17), induces the death of his only heir. On the day of his marriage to Isabella, Manfred finds his son's body: 'what a sight for a father's eyes! – He beheld his child dashed to pieces, and almost buried under an enormous helmet' (p. 19). The union between Isabella and Conrad is prevented by the supernatural presence of the helmet from Alfonso's statue. As Manfred says to Isabella, '"think no more of him," interrupted Manfred, "he was a sickly puny child, and heaven has perhaps taken him away that I might not trust the honours of my house on so frail a foundation. The line of Manfred calls for numerous supports"' (p. 24). His speedy dismissal of Conrad's death (he is not even buried) suggests Manfred's desperation, which does not allow for emotions to interfere with his plans to marry Isabella himself. As this marriage does not come to fruition either, the prevention of union through marriage ensures that there cannot be a fifth generation to inherit the illegal ownership of Otranto. As Father Jerome suggests, '"a tyrant's race must be swept from the earth to the third and fourth generation"' (p. 94). This is also the case for Matilda, who is denied union with her beloved Theodore in her dying hour. In his grief, Theodore exclaims '"Father! Jerome! Will you not join our hands?" … "why distracted rashness?" said Jerome: "is this an hour for marriage?"' (p. 111). Although his father has the power to unite his son with the woman he loves, Jerome denies them a final moment of happiness: '"it is sinful", replied the friar, "to cherish those whom heaven has doomed to destruction"' (p. 94). Like her doomed brother, Matilda dies before a marriage can take place, suffering for her ancestor's crimes. Although Manfred and Hippolita suffer for their ancestor's behaviour, they are not killed and remain in a convent at the end of the text. It is the fourth generation that suffer for their ancestor's sins; the poison that initiated a time 'out of joint' revisits the ensuing generations after the illegal event took place. As Theodore asks, '"will heaven visit the innocent for the crimes of the guilty?"' (p. 94)

Unlike Hamlet, Bret – like Manfred – is a father himself. Because of Bret's struggle with drugs and alcohol,[39] he does not acknowledge his son Robby and is not involved in the first eleven years of his life. As Jayne comments to their marriage counsellor: "'he hasn't connected with Robby'" (p. 288). After Bret is reintroduced to his son, Robby tells his father: "'everything changed when you came into the house'" (p. 328). As a result, father and son have an irreconcilable relationship. Bret is situated as both father and son in this text, with neither relationship a success. As such, his legacy is compromised by his son, who is described as a 'sad, alert boy who gave evasive answers to questions I felt demanded clarity and precision' (p. 42). Although related by blood, father and son, bound by a poisonous link, exist uncomfortably in relation to one another. Again, as Jayne remarks, "'he wasn't here when Robby was growing up . . . that's why he's just this boy to you'" (p. 288). During the same counselling session, Bret admits: "'I didn't want a kid!'" (p. 291). Although he claims he does not want a child, the linearity of inheritance is enforced on Bret who becomes deeply concerned with a loss of legacy. 'So many children were missing that it bordered on an epidemic. About a dozen boys had disappeared since I arrived in July – only boys' (p. 82). Bret's insecurities are justified as several young boys in the area are missing, vanishing 'without a trace'. However, it is only after Bret arrives that the boys begin to go missing: through the presence of the father, sons disappear. Like Manfred, Bret the father simultaneously produces and destroys his offspring. This warning is not recognized by Bret as an image of his own inadequacy as a parent and the poisonous lineage he is subject to.

After Robby also goes missing, Bret enters his bedroom, describing it as a 'showroom. Everything was exact. And it felt empty' (p. 307). It is only after Robby has vanished that Bret begins to decipher the signs of his son's unhappiness, and his own (inherited) failure as a father. In this way, the depiction of his room is a textual space for Bret to decipher: 'his desk was immaculate. The pillows on the leather sofa had no indentations on them. Every surface was clean. The room smelled of varnish and lemon' (p. 307). Uncannily, the cleanliness of the room is horrific as Bret has no remainders of his son, yet it also suggests no trail of inherited poison. By displaying his room like a showroom, Robby attempts to erase himself. In a conversation with his father, Robby remarks that "'the stars you see in the night sky actually do not exist'" (p. 424). In code, Robby tells his father that appearances are deceptive. Although he lives in the same house as his father, Robby is not living the life his father assumes. After realizing that 'no one had ever lived' in his son's room, Bret notes that 'there was something horribly wrong about this' (p. 307). For Bret, the ultimate horror is the realization that Robby had been 'putting on a performance' (p. 237) throughout. Like the act of inheritance, the son is revealed to be an illusion. 'I realised that this had been a scene so rehearsed that I could predict the last lines' (p. 239). Instead of a son, Robby is a carefully rehearsed actor, saying only what Bret wanted to hear until the day he can escape. In this way, legacy is little more than a performance, a duty that forces the son and father to act in a particular way. Just as the 'living room might as well have been a screen and the house a theatre' (p. 401), the theatrical refers to the behaviour enforced upon Bret, Hamlet and Manfred. As Bret observes, 'one entire wall was a stark black-and-white photo mural of a deserted skate park' (p. 131). Just as the living room is a 'screen', the bedroom wall is the theatrical backdrop for the performance Robby has executed. The covering of a wall with an absent space reiterates Robby's desire for freedom and erasure, a desire that he has inherited from Bret. Through a coded conversation about being drafted into the authoritative structure of the military against his will, Bret advises Robby to 'run away' (p. 240). To break the line of inheritance, Robby has no choice but to escape before the poison of his lineage can engulf him. As Bret admits, "'I don't think the father ever needs to be there ... People are better off without them'" (p. 293). Unlike Matilda, Conrad and Hamlet, Robby saves himself and demonstrates the horror of an impossible inheritance. Significantly, the three generations of Ellises have the same name: Robert, Bret, and Robby are variants of one another, cryptic signatures suggesting – like the names Hamlet and Old Hamlet – the poisonous links within their shared bloodline.

After his disappearance, Bret finds the words: 'DIssapPEAR HEre' (p. 425) scrawled on Robby's bedroom wall. As a rebellion against the system of inheritance, Robby insists on an erased history, a renewal of identity indicated by his desire to disappear. As his counsellor reminds Bret, 'the main reason you are here is to find ways to get to know your son. That is essential. That is necessary. That you connect with your son' (p. 128). In his obsession with his own father's demands, Bret dismisses his son, and his opportunity to secure a lineage fails. Instead of leaving a legacy for his son, as his own father had, Bret is left with his memories and a 'dark throne' (p. 446), a shrine for Robby that replicates the shrine his father had for him. A throne suggests authority and monarchy, an ironic emblem as Bret is left powerless at the end of the text. Like Manfred in *The Castle of Otranto*, the father has lost his chance for legacy. Although devastated by Robby's disappearance, Bret realizes 'the damage that a father can do to a son' (p. 447). Through his bizarre behaviour and return to drugs and alcohol, Bret's marriage to Jayne breaks down and the house is sold. By acting as his father demands, Bret dismisses not only his son, but (like Hamlet) his lover also. Like Ophelia and Hippolita, Jayne destroys herself in her allegiance to Bret: 'the process of the divorce struck me as fairly meaningless as we had hardly been married in the first place' (p. 443). The father has destroyed the son's ability to love. In following the father, Bret's actions destroy his own family as a time 'out of joint' is not set right. Instead, like Hamlet, Bret loses all his loved ones, resulting in a sense of desolation and paranoia: 'I reached in my raincoat and touched the gun lodged there that I now carried with me everywhere' (p. 444). Like Old Hamlet, Bret allows the poison to be poured into his ears through the destructive words of the father which reduce his life to ash. Although, like Manfred, Bret survives, he ages overnight – 'my hair had turned completely white' (p. 440) – and he is addicted to drugs – 'it was hard for me to stay awake because of the heroin I was now taking daily' (p. 443). As an intravenous drug, heroin acts as *pharmakon*, a 'beneficial' poison injected to usurp the poison Bret has inherited. In this way, Bret is punished with the horrors of life rather than the escape of death. After Bret loses everything, he lives with 'a young sculptor named Mike Graves' (p. 444). By living with a man, Bret ensures he can never again become a father, just as Manfred's banishment to a 'neighbouring convent'[40] ensures the same. Through the interference of the supernatural, it is the poison of inheritance that creates a time 'out of joint', and not usurpations of power or inaccurate inheritances. After Robby is lost, Bret writes how 'lightning would awake me from nightmares and twisting in bed I would . . . moan my son's name' (p. 445). Unlike Hamlet, Bret is forced to endure the poison that he has inherited, and in an uncanny replication of his own father, he must relive the horror of losing his son. Caught forever in the cycle of dislocated and dislocating inheritance, Bret is haunted by his son in a time that will always be 'out of joint', a time that can never be set right.

6

Gothic Currency: Mortgage, Debt and Exchange in Beyond Black

∽

This chapter explores the notion of Gothic currency, a focus on the financial obligations incurred in death. As a time of inheritance and therefore exchange, death (for ghosts and the living) is bound up with the legalities (and illegalities) of financial transactions. Such transfers indicate the associations between the law, finance and space as located through the pact of mortgage. For example, the legal inhabitant of a house is understood through her contractual obligations to the law. Through the etymology of 'mortgage', the implications of such a contract can be assessed. As a 'dead pledge', a mortgage suggests a transaction of currency bound to a particular site in return for an eternal promise, a contract until death. Such an obligation is evaluated in this chapter as a bind that continues after death. Through the occupation of familiar spaces, the ghost is bound into both spatial and financial anxieties, situating them firmly within a legal discourse. Like the law, the spectres of this text enforce a contract with the living, a simultaneously legal and illegal act. Through the exercise of an illegal legality, spectral figures are both within the law and unquestionably outside it.[1] Through spectral mortgage, the law operates through the living and the dead, dissolving the very binary opposites (right and wrong, legal and illegal) that support its status as ruling edict.

The protagonist of *Beyond Black* is a psychic named Alison who travels around London attending psychic conferences for the public. The ghost holds monetary value for Alison since she makes a living from dealing with the dead. However, her assistant Colette is blind to the ghosts that both she and Alison live amongst. In her trade, Alison must negotiate with spectres from her own past, one of which is her 'guide' Morris who follows Alison everywhere: 'He would follow you to the lavatory if he was in that sort of mood.'[2] Along with Morris, Alison is constantly surrounded by a group of spectres she describes as 'fiends', figures from her abusive past. By attempting to live in death through their occupation of familiar spaces, spectres gather around Alison for reassurance. And yet her debt to the spectres is a heavy one as without the ghosts that surround her, she could not make a living. The presence of the fiends is a constant reminder of Alison's traumatic and abusive childhood. In an attempt to remove the fiends from her life, Alison must seek the unfamiliar, a site away from the discomfiting familiarity of the spectres that haunt her, and move into a new house. In doing so, Alison and Colette are bound into a spectral contract, an il/legal mortgage (funded by spectres) that leaves them further indebted to the spectres that surround them.

By making a living from the dead, Alison's existence is determined through her interaction with spectres; the ghost has thus become a commodity. The spectrality of exchange is explored by Derrida in *Specters of Marx*. As he highlights, 'Marx always described money, and more precisely the monetary sign, in the figure of appearance or simulacrum, more exactly of the ghost'.[3] Like the ghost, money is a present absence, a figure that substitutes itself for the value it signifies. Hence, money always functions like text, through a signifier: signified relationship as an effect of the distance between the monetary sign and the value it purports to designate. In relation to Saussure, Derrida suggests that 'a word can be exchanged for something dissimilar, an idea . . . its value is therefore not fixed so long as one simply states that it can be "exchanged" for a given concept'.[4] Through the metaphor of exchange, the signs of money and text can be aligned with the unstable sign of the ghost. Money is also inscribed with text, bound through the stamp of the law: 'inscription on coinage is most often the intersection, the scene of the exchange between the linguistic and the economic.'[5] Due to the fluctuating exchange value of money, the coin is inscribed with a sign of permanence; although the value may change, the object is fixed with the official stamp of the law. As Derrida elaborates, 'the spectral virtue of money [suggests] money [is] the origin both of spirit and of avarice'.[6]

Like the process of financial exchange, the transfer of signifiers for signification positions language as a similarly economic transaction. After explaining that spectres do not take up room in the usual way, Colette responds to Alison with: "'No. Of course not. It's the way you talk about them." Alison replies, "I can't think how else to talk. I only have the usual words.""[7] Alison cannot explain the ghosts to Colette as she only has the words available to her in language. Such a language does not articulate the ghost and so there are no terms available to explain its occupation of space. Therefore its position, or value, within language cannot be expressed or exchanged. This is also demonstrated by Alison in her role as psychic, as instead of telling the public the truth about the world of the dead, Alison weaves a narrative to help people understand. The narrative she has produced is an idealistic one, a description that the living can understand. 'Spirit world, as Al describes it to the trade, is a garden, or to be more accurate a public place in the open air: litter-free like an old-fashioned park, with a bandstand in a heat haze in the distance. Here the dead sit in rows on benches' (p. 43). The creation of orderly rows suggests that Alison is imposing legality to produce an acceptable image of the spectre. More importantly, though, she is positioning the ghost through signifiers that can be exchanged and therefore understood.

Just as the residents of Admiral Drive monitor the presence of the homeless, Alison suggests that the dead should also be monitored, and yet there are no notices to warn against such apparitions. Such signs would be meaningless as the position of the spectre is one that cannot be articulated or exchanged through language. Alison comments that 'outside there are notices affixed to poles, warning of hawkers, peddlers, itinerant sellers and illegal traders. There are none that warn against the loose, travelling dead' (p. 238). By aligning the dead with traders, Alison associates them with exchange, the distribution of goods for profit. The warning indicated by the sign, however, suggests an illegal trade, an exchange not accounted for within the law. Like the ghost's refusal to signify through language, its position within the law is not accounted for as the ghost simply cannot be exchanged. As suggested in *Given Time*, 'the law of economy is the − circular − return to the point of departure, to the origin, also to the home'.[8] Instead of the conventional, linear exchange of finance,

Derrida suggests that the law of economy is circular. Like the ghost, currency perpetually returns. Like haunting, money spent is involved in a cycle of exchange as legal tender is never fixed in value.

Just as the laws of economy and haunting are aligned with the circular, the exchange of signifiers for signification can also be understood as cyclical. As explored in chapter 1, the transfer of signifiers results in further dissemination of signifiers. As Alison reflects upon her schooldays, she remembers how spectres would materialize and 'master the pen and write gibberish' (p. 114). Spectral control of a signifying device is suggestive as the spectre highlights the disintegration of language. She remarks that

> if she'd got a few words down safely, she preferred to go over them with her blue ballpoint, branding the letters well into the paper: then drawing daisy petals around the 'o's and giving the 'g's little fishy faces. This was dull but it was better to be bored than to risk letting the gibberish in by an unguarded stroke, branching out into white space. (p. 115)

Therefore, the values exchanged by the spectres have no transactional value as their signifiers are just 'gibberish'. Alison remarks that 'You had to guard the words that came out of your mouth and even the words as they formed up in your mind' (p. 321). Alison is banished from the classroom because of this spectral interference, reinforcing the ghosts' ability to determine the spaces she occupies: 'the lesson is scripture and she is thrown out to stand in the corridor' (p. 421). For Alison, being haunted results in a binding contract of debt, but also repeated exclusion: like an uninvited guest or parasite, she is persistently expelled from spaces. Because she is illegally bound to that which does not signify, every space becomes a haunted one, a realm where she is not welcome.

The correlation of money and the spectral can be understood through debt. In death, an inevitable debt arises for the spectre, as estates, houses and materials are passed on to the next of kin. As Derrida writes in *The Ear of the Other*,

> at the very least, to be dead means that no profit or deficit, no good or evil, whether calculated or not, can *ever return again* to the bearer

of the name. Only the name can inherit, and this is why the name, to be distinguished from the bearer, is always and a priori a dead man's name, a name of death.[9]

After death, only the living can inherit, and therefore the spectre loses everything that its living incarnation had owned in life. The obsession with loss is evident in this text through the attempt of the spectres to secure themselves via legal contracts. Such a concern is apparent in classic Gothic texts such as *The Castle of Otranto* where the determination to ensure inheritance is proclaimed by both the living and the dead.

The alignment of spectres with finance is explored overtly throughout *Beyond Black*, as Alison openly acknowledges her debt to the spectres that surround her: 'I lived with them, they lived with me, my childhood was spent in the half-light, waiting for my talent to develop and my means of making a living, knowing always, knowing always I owed my existence to them' (p. 347). Because of this, Alison gains a haunting credit that simultaneously reminds her of a spectral debt. Stability is impossible in this spectral finance, as where there is credit there must always be debt. For example, the money earned through spectral communication provides Alison with a new house. Through a cyclical economy, the spectral fiends provide Alison with a house that they will haunt. Such dependence suggests a loan or mortgage that must be repaid to the spectres on their demand. After Alison and Colette move into the Collingwood, Morris remarks: '"This is posh, innit? You're doing very well out of me, ducks"' (p. 245). Such a mortgage binds Alison to the spectres further, providing them with the authority of ownership. As Derrida writes in *Specters of Marx*, 'the miser, the hoarder, the speculator becomes a martyr to exchange-value'.[10] Through her contractual debt, Alison falls prey to the spectres that control it.

In death, the spectres that follow Alison are obsessed with financial matters. In particular, Morris is fixated on retrieving what he is owed: '"the day I was taken over, there wasn't five bob in my pocket. I was taken over and I don't know how, taken over wiv money owing to me." Morris began to whimper. "MacArthur owes me. Bill Wagstaffe owes me. I've got it in my little black book who owes me"' (p. 412). The money he is still owed suggests that debt persists after death as the weight of a legal contract still exerts its power. Such autonomy is assisted by the similarities between the spectre and money. As Derrida highlights, the ghosts are 'apparition[s] of the bodiless body of money: not the lifeless body or the cadaver, but a life without personal life or individual property ... the monetary specter, value, money or its fiduciary sign, gold'.[11] Morris's preoccupation with debt is expressed in legal terms, as although he is not living, he still wants his money lawfully returned. 'When he thought of the debts he had incurred, of the injuries done and what was rightfully owed to him, he would run after Alison, agitated: after his hostess, his missus' (p. 164). The ability of the law to bind is so powerful that the chain is unbroken after death, suggesting the illegality of the law itself. The pathway of the law is a continuous line that (illegally) never fails to operate. This persistence (of debt) highlights the spectral utility of legality, as through the legal charter of the mortgage, the outlawed spectre acts both within and outside the law in a display of *différance*. In this way, the spectre is still shackled to life, still part of a contractual mortgage that binds it to familiar spaces.

As Alison and Colette travel around the M25 from venue to venue, there are certain places that Alison would rather not go through. As Alison drives through large conurbations, she can see groups of confused spectres, struggling to adjust to the state of death.

> They tried to avoid the high streets and shopping malls of the denatured towns, because of the bewildered dead clustered among the skips outside the burger bars, clutching door keys in their hands, or queuing with their lunch boxes where the gates of small factories once stood where machines once whirred and chugged behind sooty panes of old glass. (p. 265)

Such spectres are in search of the familiar to reassure them of their state of existence. The 'clutching of door keys' and 'lunch boxes' suggests they remain bound to an economy of work within a capitalist society. Just as money is an issue in life, these spectres are concerned with returning to work. In doing so, they are reassured that they have a familiar site to inhabit that ensures that they have an exchange-value, that their labour is still worth something. This demonstrates how the economy of work persists after death, producing spectres that are bound to a legal system of finance and space.

As Georges Perec remarks in his essay 'Species of spaces', 'space is reassurance'.[12] Spectres utilize familiar spaces in order to reassure themselves that they still operate within a system of legal, spatial and financial signification. As Mark Wigley suggests, '*Being and Time* argued that the familiar everyday world is precisely a "fleeing in the face of uncanniness" that "suppresses everything unfamiliar"'.[13] As an image of security, the familiar attempts to determine everything as familiar, to suppress the uncanniness of the unfamiliar. After Alison moves from her familiar flat to an unfamiliar new house, Morris objects: '"he doesn't like it, you see. Says it's not a proper home"' (p. 239). For Morris, the new and unfamiliar are not homely as he is no longer bound to a site associated with his past as one of the living. '"How can I move," he said, "when I have given out this as my address? How will Nick find me, how will my old mates know where to come?"' (p. 227). This spatial anxiety demonstrates the spectre's desire for fixity, for an address. Without a familiar base, Morris will lose the comfort of being bound within a signifying system, a union secured through space but also through the other. As Alison observes,

> There are thousands of them out there, so pathetic and lame-brained they can't cross the road to get where they're going, dithering on the kerbs of new arterial roads and bypasses, as the vehicles swish by: congregating under railway arches and under the stairwells of multi-storey car parks, thickening the air at the entrance to underground stations. (p. 265)

The text suggests that spectres are not solitary but part of a gathering,[14] with the chances of being reunited with someone they know as 'about the same as meeting somebody you know at a main-line station at rush hour' (p. 33). The vastness of their number suggests a reassurance through gathering, a clinging on to the familiar. Just as life binds individuals to one another, the bond continues after death, as indicated by Morris's desire to be found by his friends. As Derrida suggests, ghosts are part of a community, 'some population of ghosts'.[15] Because of this, the spectres in this text experience spatial anxiety, a consideration for those 'taking up room'.

Like the ghosts, Alison and Colette spend a lot of time travelling to and from different venues for psychic conferences. Like the cyclical nature of haunting, finance and signification, Alison's repetitive journeys round the M25 motorway indicate the circular web she is caught in. Because of this, they have to stay in hotels at several locations. Occupying hotels is rather problematic for Alison, however, as she can decipher the historical violence inscribed in such spaces. She remarks how

> there's a lot of sadness in hotel rooms, soaked up by the soft furnishings: a lot of loneliness and guilt and regret. A lot of ghosts too: whiskery chambermaids stumping down the corridors on their bad legs, tippling night porters who've collapsed on the job, guests who've drowned in the bath or suffered a stroke in their beds. (p. 41)

With her extraordinary sight, Alison can read the scars of history that remain in spaces. Structures such as walls and doors saturate the trauma that has occurred within them as the past is bound to space. As Mark Wigley writes, 'spaces cannot be cleansed of violence'.[16] The violence of living (and dying) is scored in space, and Alison has the ability to decipher such signs. In the Foreword to Bachelard's *Poetics of Space*, John R. Stilgoe remarks how Bachelard 'probes the impact of human habitation on geometrical form, and the impact of the form upon human inhabitants'.[17] He suggests that spaces are changed by the humans that occupy them through the events and emotions experienced there. Through a legal and financial contract, inhabitants are bound to the spaces they occupy. When Alison arrives at a regularly used site (such as the hotel), she has to 'regurgitate or else digest all the distress that she's sucked in from the carpet and the walls' (p. 29). Alison is able to detect lines of violence in any space that has experienced a variety of people and events, and hence her decision to move to a new house allows her to avoid traumas from the past. As Alison remarks: "'I'd like to live nowhere'" (p. 221). In contrast to the ghost of Morris who desires a specific address, Alison desires no address, a place that is not even on a map. This desire signifies her attempt to extricate herself from her past, to unravel her legal binding to spectres and the debt she is collapsing under. In his discussion of *The Eighteenth Brumaire* in *Specters of Marx*, Derrida suggests that 'if death weighs on the living brain of the living, it must then have some spectral density. To weigh is also to charge.'[18] Through the weight of the past, the spectral is associated with a heavy debt (both of substance and weightlessness) that is inherited.

The 'housing' of the past has been examined by Derrida in *Archive Fever: A Freudian Impression*, where he evaluates how the past is chained to the site that surrounds it. In her book *Dust*, Carolyn Steedman suggests that archive fever

> starts in the early hours of the morning, in the bed of a cheap hotel, where the historian cannot get to sleep. You cannot get to sleep because you lie so narrowly, in an attempt to avoid contact with anything that isn't shielded by sheets and pillowcase. The first sign then, is an excessive attention to the bed, an irresistible anxiety about the hundreds who have slept there before you, leaving their dust and debris in the fibres of the blankets, greasing the surface of the heavy, slippery counterpane. The dust of others, and of other times, fills the room, settles on the carpet, marks out the sticky passage from bed to bathroom.[19]

As Steedman explains, traces of others determine space and overwhelm the (living) inhabitant to induce a kind of fever. The violence of existence inscribes a subversive pathway, a 'sticky passage' indicating the movement of an uncanny other rendered both dead and alive. As Wigley suggests, 'there is no violence without institution, no institution without space, no space without violence'.[20] Alison's visit to a hotel results in 'an exhausting hour tussling with an old corpse in a sheet' (p. 41). Not only does a ghost hound Alison in her bed, but the pasts that are linked to the ghost and the many others in the hotel haunt her simultaneously. Her fear of sleeping in certain places is symptomatic of archive fever: 'when they check into a room Alison stands on the threshold and sniffs the atmosphere, inhales it' (p. 41). Alison's detection of signs begins with the threshold, an indication of others who have crossed into the space. Steedman adds that 'you think, in the delirium: it was their dust that I breathed in'.[21] In Alison's case, the signs she deciphers begin to mark her own body as she absorbs the violence around her. She hopes that by keeping the house clean 'she and Colette, between them, could keep down the lower sort, who drift in dust-rolls under beds' (pp. 270–1). Such violence is described as dust, cinder remains that linger within space.

As Steedman suggests: '*nothing goes away* . . . the past has deposited all of its traces, somewhere, somehow.'[22] Traces of the past cannot be removed as their debt to space is to be contained within it. This is also the case for Alison: '"I am a settlement, a place of safety, a bomb-proof shelter"' (p. 347). Her body has become a structure that houses, a space that absorbs violence in a binding to the past. Through such ingestion, Alison aligns herself with a sewage worker: 'my clients won't do their dirty work. They want it contracted out. They write me a cheque for thirty quid and expect me to clear their drains' (p. 183). Alison's trade is also to ingest people's trauma, and then expel the remainder of their painful pasts. Like the process of mourning explored in chapter 4, Alison's interaction with the dead involves a system of conjuration, digestion and expulsion. However, after Alison moves into her new home, there is a problem with the sewage system.

> At Admiral Drive a few people phoned the local environmental health department, putting questions about the play area, but officials would only admit to some sort of blockage, some sort of seepage. . . . the populace was restless and transient, and already the first 'For Sale' signs were going up, as footloose young couples tried their luck in a rising market. (p. 252)

The seepage of dirt into the housing estate represents a hidden remainder that has resurfaced, a substance that should have been digested and expelled. The failure of this system reinforces the text's focus on circularity and the return of what has been exchanged.

Although new, the building site of Admiral Drive is permeated with signs of violence: 'she sensed the underscape, shuddering as it waited to be ripped. Builders' machines stood ready, their maws crusted with soil, waiting for Monday morning. Violence hung in the air, like the smell of explosives. Birds had flown. Foxes had abandoned their lairs' (p. 218). Like the lines of violence present in buildings such as schools, houses and hotels, the ground that will be built upon is also inscribed with violence. The act of building is violent, not only to the wildlife but also to the ground itself. By building over this land, the space is 'housed', contained and controlled in a violent manner. After the buildings are sold, the estate of houses represents a trail of fetters that bind the occupants to the law. This binding is achieved through conveyancing, the transfer of property in which the law mediates between buyer and seller. In selling the houses, the law is witness to an exchange process that binds, a violence that originates with the law. As Derrida proposes in his essay, 'Force of law: the mystical foundation of authority', 'the origin of authority, the foundation or ground, the position of the law can't by definition rest on anything but themselves, they are themselves a violence without ground'.[23] Such violence ensures that the legal subject is always within the law. Suzi, the estate agent, remarks that as building begins, '"we'll have to wear helmets when we go out there. It'll be mud up to your knees. Like a battlefield"' (p. 216). Her language of war describes the action of building but also the violent imposition of the law on such building. The imagery of war evokes the victory of the law over the subject: the threat to the individual is clear from the necessity of helmets.

> That summer, the birch trees were cut down and the last birds flew away. Their song was replaced by the roaring of road drills, the beeping of the JCBs backing up, the cursing of carriers and the cries of the wounded, and scrubland gave way to a gashed landscape of trenches and moats, of mud chutes and standing pools of yellow water. (p. 226)

Like a battlefield, the ground will be covered with trenches, where each (potential) homeowner must fight for the right to possess land. As Wigley suggests, spaces are embedded with violence through the economy of building: 'the economy of violence inscribed into spaces that constitute them as such'.[24] Through building, finance and violence are inextricably linked to the legality of an exchange process that is never truly an exchange. As Alison demonstrates, mortgage insists upon the submission of the applicant to the enormity of debt.

When Alison moves into the house at Admiral Drive, she wants '"Somewhere clean. Somewhere new. A house that nobody's lived in before"' (p. 199). Although the house is new and empty, it is full of structural mistakes: 'a couple of the internal doors being hung the wrong way round, inside out and the Adam-style fireplace being off centre' (p. 228). Because the hearth is off centre, the entire house is dislocated, as without a pivot point the space of the house is misaligned.

The violence of Alison's past follows her into her new home, and although new, the house contains impressions of her traumatic life. The exchange she hoped for has not taken place as the trauma of her past has not been expelled. The ground of the second floor is destroyed when 'their kitchen ceiling fell in' (p. 228), indicating the weight of Alison's past but also that of mortgage. Her desire to live 'nowhere' is thwarted by the power of the past to invade space. In an attempt to escape the ghosts that are bound to her in law and space, Alison actually brings the weight of her past with her. 'When the men came to take the pine dresser away, he (Morris) lay on top of it to make it heavy. He infiltrated Al's mattress and infused his spirit sulks among the fibres, so that it bucked and rippled in the men's hands and they almost dropped it in alarm' (p. 227). After signing the mortgage contract, her past is impressed upon the new house as 'the tradition of all the dead generations weighs like a nightmare on the brain of the living'.[25] This weight is imposed upon the house itself, as Alison's heavy past is housed within her large body that 'flattens' the stair carpet so much that is needs replacing. 'Alison was a woman who seemed to fill a room, even when she wasn't in it. She was of an unfeasible size, with plump creamy shoulders, rounded calves, thighs and hips that overflowed her chair' (p. 3). As Colette remarks to Alison: '"All those marks rubbed along the walls. Do you know you leave a mark? Wherever your shoulders touch it"' (p. 283). The once new house has been contaminated by Alison's past and the events that have taken place there. As Derrida writes: 'To weigh is also to charge, tax, impose, indebt, accuse, assign, enjoin.'[26] The weight of her past is a spectral mass that exerts itself through the law of mortgage, the binding of a person to the familiarity of her past. 'She sees, back at Admiral Drive, the tape unspooling in the empty house, her past unspooling, back beyond this life, beyond the lives to come' (p. 442). Her history will be contained in the house, ready for the next inhabitants also to make their mark on it. As Wigley writes, 'it is only the poet's exile from the home that can establish its strange condition, the unfamiliarity of its apparently familiar enclosure'.[27] Like the heaviness of the spectres that follow Alison, the house is only owned through a contractual borrowing agreed to by the law. *Specters of Marx* suggests that 'inheritance from the "spirits of the past" consists, as always, in borrowing. Figures of

borrowing, borrowed figures, figurality as the figure of borrowing.'[28]
To borrow is to be haunted, by debt but also the law.

Just as her new home becomes indicative of her past traumas,
Alison's childhood home is inscribed with lines of violence.

> The roof leaked, and black mould drew a drippy, wavering line down
> one corner. The house was a mess. Bits were continually falling off it.
> You'd get left with the door handle in your hand, and when somebody
> put a fist through a window one night it got mended with cardboard
> and stayed like that. (p. 100)

The violence of the inside of the house (abuse, prostitution, murder)
is displayed on the house's exterior. The 'wavering line' suggests an
impossible pathway, a line of violence that is inscribed in the space.
In addition, the house's inability to remain whole represents an extreme
violence within that dismantles the structure's ability to house. Trauma
scars the house both inside and out through the violence of the past
and the inevitable legal binding of house to person: 'the doors banged,
and sometimes the windows smashed' (p. 100). Because of the house's
violent history, it is bulldozed to the ground. As Alison dictates to
the spirit of Mrs Etchells: '"they've demolished those houses . . .
where my mum used to live, it's a big car showroom now"' (p. 375).
Her childhood home has been replaced with a showroom, and hence
Alison's lineage is also dismantled into a disjointed line of ancestry
that she cannot trace. Although haunted by and illegally bound to
her past through spectral interaction, her past does not include a
father: Alison cannot trace her roots to ascertain her true inheritance.
Instead, she remains indebted to the trauma of a past she does not
fully understand.

Disjointed ancestry[29] is introduced through the figure of Colette,
who, the first time she meets Alison, is told some shocking news:
'"Terry's your uncle, and Uncle Mike's your dad"' (p. 83). Through
her extended sight, Alison reveals that Colette's lineage is confused
as the man she had thought was her uncle is in fact her father. This
is read through the cufflinks that Colette had bought her father for
Christmas, a remainder of her father that Alison can decipher. When
Colette finds out her family secret, her response is in financial terms:
'he'd paid, but he hadn't paid enough, he'd paid as an uncle, but not

as a dad. I'll sue the bastard, she thought' (p. 87). Just as the spectres are intimately connected to finance, Colette responds to her dislocated lineage through money and the law. Like the spectres, Colette is determined to receive what she is owed: not a father, but the money he owes her. Because the space we occupy binds us to the past (a binding achieved through the law, space and mortgage), Colette understands her missing father as a debt owed: 'she did look like a woman who had lost her money: lost her lottery ticket in life, lost her dad and lost her home' (p. 92). Because he was absent during her past, Colette requires some form of compensation or exchange to make up for the loss. In the space of absence comes the figure of money. Colette's obsession with finance increases when she becomes Alison's 'business brain', as Alison 'hadn't even registered for VAT . . . as for income tax, her allowances were all over the place' (p. 94). Because of her debt to the spectral, Alison is not in line with the law.

As Alison remarks, 'it was not uncommon to find family memory so short, in these towns where nobody comes from, these south-eastern towns with their floating populations and their car parks where the centre should be' (pp. 16–17). The same is true for Alison, who has never known her father. In response to Alison's questions, her mother replies: "'I dunno, girl. I would help you, if I could. It could be any one of 'em, or it could be six other fellas'" (p. 435). Her search for lineage is thwarted by her lack of documentation: "'I don't even have a birth certificate", Al said. "Not that I know of. To be honest, I'm not really sure how old I am'" (p. 401). Because there is no paperwork with the official stamp of the law, Alison is unrecorded, and hence unlocatable. Alison is not bound to her parents through the law; instead she is bound to the men that she grew up with through a lineage of violence and trauma. Although she is not legally recorded, Alison is still a subject of the law, bound into the space of her past through the inextricable link between law and space.

Her lineage is further confused by her grandparentage, as a psychic named Mrs Etchells claims her son fathered Alison and that she is her grandmother. These claims, however, are never validated. After her death, Mrs Etchells provides Alison's 'name as next of kin' (p. 374), although after going to her home, 'nothing was left but a square of patterned carpet that didn't quite meet the sides of the room' (p. 397). After Mrs Etchells dies, Alison hopes to find something in her home indicating her lineage and decides to search her house.

> There was a crack, a splintering, floorboards showed, she saw a small piece of paper, folded. She bent painfully to scoop it up. She unfolded it, and as she did so the fibres of the paper gave way, and it fell apart along the folds. My birth certificate, she thought: but no, it was barely six lines. (p. 404)

Because Alison has no documentation that legally records her existence, she hopes her (supposed) grandmother has retained something to reaffirm her 'official' status. In finding a crack in the floorboards, Alison locates a crypt, a space where something is hidden for safe keeping. Instead of finding herself or an official version of herself, she finds an indication of debt.

> First a blurred rubber stamp: PAID TO. Then *Emmeline Cheetham* was written beneath, in a florid, black hand: *The Sum of Seven Shillings and Sixpence.* Underneath came another stamp, at an angle to the above, RECEIVED WITH THANKS: and then in her mother's youthful hand, her signature, *Emmeline Cheetham:* below that, IN WITNESS THEREOF: *Irene Etchells (Mrs).* Beneath the signature, the paper had a brown indentation, as if it had been ironed briefly on a high setting. As the nail of her little finger touched the scorch mark, the paper flaked away, leaving a ragged gap where the mark had been. (p. 404)

Again, through her desperation to receive, Alison is burdened with further debt. As Mrs Etchells dies intestate, her death results in a negative value, a cyclical return of a debt whose transaction took place many years ago. As Derrida explores in *Paper Machine:* 'Credit or discredit, legitimation and delegitimation, have long been signified by the body of paper. A guarantee is worth what a signed piece of paper is worth.'[30] The paper signifies the weight of the legal contract between the individual subject and the law, as well as the alignment of paper with money. Derrida states that 'when the State emits paper money at a fixed rate, its intervention is compared to "magic" that transmutes paper into gold'.[31] Paper has been exchanged as money and therefore acts as both money and witness. As the surface for inscription or signification, paper functions as a vehicle for exchange, indicating both legal contract and debt.

Alison's desire for a new house is induced by her dislocated sense of lineage and belonging. In discussion with Colette, Alison remarks: "'Why not? It's a nice little flat but I've got no roots here'" (p. 199). She moves in an attempt to release her bond to the past and remove the fiendish ghosts from her life: "'If we moved, we might be able to lose them'" (p. 201). After Colette's agreement, they begin to look at the plans of a housing estate called Admiral Drive. As Colette reminds Alison: "'You have to go back beyond paint finishes and colour schemes, back beyond bricks and mortar, look at the ground we'll be standing on. It isn't just a place to live. It's an investment. We need to maximise the profit'" (p. 218). In their search for a new home, Colette reminds Alison that the house will be another form of income for the pair. Alison must therefore consider the exchange value of the ground they will be investing in, land that will legally bind them to the site.

As Alison looks around the site, she remarks: "'It's a field. There's nothing here'" (p. 221), to which Colette responds: "'You have to imagine them [the houses]'" (p. 221). In buying a house that has not yet been built, Alison is exchanging money for a vacant plot of land, highlighting that "'it's not even on a map, is it?'" (p. 221). Colette responds by stating that "'they'll redraw the map, in time'" (p. 221). In its pre-built state, the house is spectral, akin to a spectre before materialization. Like the potential of all houses to be haunted, all land has the potential for building. The sales assistant exchanges empty ground for money, and yet the mortgage agreement imposes a weight upon Alison and Colette, a weight shared by the other inhabitants of Admiral Drive: 'they were hardly men at all, not men as Colette knew them, they were dutiful emasculates, squat and waddling under their burden of mortgage debt' (p. 229). Before the house is even built, the weight exerted on the homeowners is the weight of the law. By signing legal documentation, Alison has official paperwork that binds her to Colette. 'I need, she thought, to give Colette more of a stake in life. Get her name on the house deeds. Give her more reason to stick around, so she's less inclined to take off in a sulk or on a whim' (p. 203). In this instance, paper represents the space of the law, but also shares in ownership. After Colette leaves Alison, she states that "'I just need to work out how to extricate myself from my ties with Alison. I may need to see a solicitor'" (p. 426). In order to release herself from the legally binding contract of mortgage, Colette must interact with the law.

Although ghosts occupy the familiar, they do not inhabit space like the living. In response to Colette, Alison remarks that "'They don't take up room in the usual way'" (p. 200). And yet the dead exhibit signs of spectral spatial anxiety, abiding by their own laws in a consideration for 'taking up space'. In a perverse extension of the laws of the living, the spectres will expel those that occupy space they are not entitled to. Therefore, the ghost is also bound up with a system of exchange that attempts expulsion. As Peter Goodrich writes, 'it was for the law to determine the truth of the sign, efficacy or force, and in doing so it would necessarily institute a governance of perception [of] the world of appearance, of images, with either the sign or the dissimulation of an unseen, "aereall" or ghostly realm'.[32] Although the law has determined the supernatural as illegal, by attempting to control the space of the dead the spectres in *Beyond Black* act according to a series of laws. From their position outside the law, the spectres mock legality by conjuring their own legal additions, becoming host to a realm they have been excluded from. As Morris remarks to Alison,

> We are chasing out all spooks what are asylum seekers, derelicts, vagrants and refugees, and clearing out all spectres unlawfully residing in attics, lofts, cupboards, cracks in the pavement and holes in the ground. All spooks with no identification will be removed. It ain't good enough to say you've nowhere to go. It ain't good enough to say that your documents fell through the hole in your breeches . . . Nobody is to take up room they ain't entitled to. Show me your entitlement or I'll show you the boot. (p. 386)

The law Morris enforces employs the same terminology as the laws of the living, indicating the spectre's desire to utilize the familiar. In this instance, Morris aligns the undocumented spectre with the refugee or the asylum seeker. As Derrida explores in *Paper Machine*, 'the question of the person with no papers, crushed by so many machines, [is futile] when we are all, already, undocumented, "paperless"'.[33] Such spectral law utilizes the legal alignment of paper and space, as through documentation, citizenship (and mortgage) is granted. The importance of paper to the spectre is as a familiar remainder, a re-assurance that it is still within a system of law that determines it as subject. Without paper, a law cannot operate, and without law there can be no subjects. By enforcing the law, Morris is involved in exiling other ghosts, casting them out of spaces they are not entitled to. Without being bound to a space through paper, the ghost becomes homeless. Even the ground and the pavement will be governed by this law; cracks, holes, lofts and cupboards will be regulated. Such spaces ensure there is not one corner available to the illegal host of a ghost, an operation that requires significant surveillance. This spatial anxiety experienced by both the dead and the living is enhanced as Alison explains that '"there are more of them than us"' (p. 373). As Colette walks into Alison's dressing room, Morris is lying across the threshold: 'when Colette stepped back she trampled straight over him' (p. 5). The lack of unoccupied space produces a realm where the dead and the living must interact: '"the floor would be all rolling over with little dead babies, you wouldn't know where to put your feet"' (p. 368).

The anxiety of space extends to the new neighbourhood where Alison and Colette live: 'Torches crept over Admiral Drive. It was the neighbourhood watch, beginning their evening search, among the cow-parsley meadows that led to the canal, for any poor wastrels or refugees who had grubbed in for the night' (p. 374). Like the spirits, the living inhabitants of Admiral Drive are concerned with unlawful residents: 'the council is taking the benches out of the park so that no one can sleep on them' (p. 318). After Alison and Colette purchase a shed, a man named Mart, 'homeless and down on his luck' (p. 297), occupies it. Hiding him from Colette and the neighbours, Alison helps Mart by feeding him and giving him money: 'he's my visitor. I can have a visitor, if I want, I suppose?' (p. 293). By housing a homeless man, Alison is breaking the law. The primary threat to Mart's occupation of the shed is not, however, from the living. After assisting in Mart's murder, the spectral Morris responds: '"he was on my manor! Only just got a proper outbuilding, where I can put me feet up evenings, and some geezer with a hat moves in"' (p. 444). It

is through the implementation of spectral law that Mart is exiled
from the space of the shed. In this way, Morris's task of 'clearing out
all spectres unlawfully residing in attics, lofts, cupboards' (p. 386) is
similar to the policing of Sergeant Delingbole and the neighbourhood
watch. Once the neighbourhood residents find out about Alison's
unlawful guest, they turn against her for encouraging the homeless
into their realm. 'She hears the neighbours chanting – OUT OUT
OUT – a swell of distant voices, like a choir' (p. 425). Because Alison
has assisted an illegal subject, the surrounding inhabitants are determined to expel her from her home. The crime of assisting the homeless becomes apparent by its financial implications. As a neighbour
complains: "'we'll be in the local paper as that place where the tramp
topped himself, and that won't be very nice for our resale values"'
(p. 409). Instead of considering the other, the neighbours are concerned about their mortgages, their debts to the law. As Derrida
suggests in *Given Time: Counterfeit Money*, 'the beggar occupies a
determined place in a social, politicoeconomic, and symbolic topology.
He does not work. *In principle*, begging produces nothing, no wealth,
no surplus-value.'[34] Due to his lack of capital, the homeless beggar
lies outside the law as he is not contracted to a home through mortgage
or finance. Hence Mart is an outlaw, and yet he is still subject to the
illegality of occupying Alison's shed.

For her crimes, Alison is ultimately arrested in her own home:
'Colette double-locked the front door and put the bolts on' (p. 408).
As Mark Wigley writes: 'House arrest is not the policing of the space
of the house but the house itself as police action or, more precisely,
police action as housing. To arrest, after all, is to domesticate by
restricting movement, defining its limits, drawing a line.'[35] By keeping
Alison and Colette under house arrest, the neighbours are securing
them within the structure of the house, binding them to their house
(and mortgage) further. By employing the house in this way, the
law of the house is highlighted and its ability to domesticate the
inhabitants is apparent. In doing so, they become spectral and occupy
the corners of the room: 'they sat with the lamps unlit, so as not to
attract the attention of the neighbours, they moved cautiously, sliding
around the edges of the room' (p. 410). In her disobedience to the
law, Alison has become monstrous and must exit her house in disguise:
"'Sergeant Delingbole says, what you could do, probably it would

be for the best, would be to come out with a blanket over your head'" (p. 441). The same is true for Colette, who insists that "'I don't intend to spend another night under this roof'" (p. 413) and leaves Admiral Drive under the disguise of night.

After Alison leaves the home she shared with Colette, she begins a new life with new spirit guides who restore her lost lineage: 'they praise her, saying that they never had a daughter, but if they had, they would have wanted a bonny big girl just like Al' (pp. 448–9). By leaving the house mortgaged to her via the spectres of her past, Alison is released from her debt to them as she refuses to interact in the exchange demanded of her. By untangling herself from her past, Alison arrives at a settlement and a sense of equilibrium. Without Colette and with her new spirit guides, her sense of self, past and legacy is reaffirmed and "'business is booming . . . give or take the odd quiet midweek. I'm booked out till next Feb'" (p. 450). Without the weight (and debt) of mortgage, Alison's financial credit increases. In escaping the spectres, she also evades legality as without a mortgage she is no longer in the law's debt.

Afterword

෨

This book demonstrates the explosive potential of examining contemporary texts through concepts that have been aligned with the Gothic. There are many other texts and themes that open themselves up to such analysis, as the concepts under discussion here are constantly being renewed, refusing to rest in peace. These potentials for renewal which refuse to locate the Gothic explain the absence of a conclusion in this book: there is far more to say on these concepts than I am capable of in six chapters. Any attempt to conclude would also be in conflict with many of the theoretical ideas explored here, as Simon Critchley suggests: 'the goal of Derrida's reading practice is to *let the remains remain*. You cannot catch the sea in your hands.'[1] Instead of an arrival, this book confidently gestures towards the to-come: as Patrick Bateman testifies, 'THIS IS NOT AN EXIT'.[2]

Notes

༄

Introduction

1   David Punter, 'The ghost of a history', in *A Companion to the Gothic* (London: Blackwell, 2001), viii.
2   Catherine Spooner, 'Introduction: Gothic in contemporary popular culture', *Gothic Studies*, 9/1 (2007), 2.
3   Alex Warwick, 'Feeling Gothicky?', *Gothic Studies*, 9/1 (2007), 6.
4   Jodey Castricano, *Cryptomimesis: The Gothic and Jacques Derrida's Ghost Writing* (London: McGill-Queen's University Press, 2001).
5   Nicholas Royle, *In Memory of Jacques Derrida* (Edinburgh: Edinburgh University Press, 2009), p. 1.
6   Jacques Derrida, *Specters of Marx: The State of the Debt, the Work of Mourning, and the New International* (London: Routledge, 1994).
7   Derrida, *The Post Card: From Socrates to Freud and Beyond* (Chicago: University of Chicago Press, 1987).
8   Derrida, *The Gift of Death* (Chicago: University of Chicago Press, 1996).
9   Derrida, *Of Hospitality: Anne Dufourmantelle invites Jacques Derrida to Respond* (Stanford, CA: Stanford University Press, 2000).
10 Derrida, *Paper Machine* (Stanford, CA: Stanford University Press, 2005).
11 Derrida, *Dissemination* (London: Continuum, 2004 [1981]).
12 Derrida, *Of Grammatology* (London: The Johns Hopkins University Press, 1997 [1974]).
13 Derrida, *Margins of Philosophy* (Chicago: University of Chicago Press, 1982).

14   Sigmund Freud, 'The uncanny', in Albert Dickson (ed.), *Art and Literature* (London: Penguin, 1990 [1919]).

15   Julia Kristeva, *Black Sun: Depression and Melancholia* (New York: Columbia University Press, 1989).

16   Emmanuel Levinas, *Totality and Infinity: An Essay on Exteriority* (The Hague and Boston: M. Nijhoff Publishers, 1979).

17   Mark Wigley, *The Architecture of Deconstruction: Derrida's Haunt* (London: MIT Press, 1993).

18   Peter Goodrich, *Oedipus Lex: Psychoanalysis, History, Law* (Berkeley: University of California Press, 1995).

19   Gideon Ofrat, *The Jewish Derrida* (Syracuse, NY: Syracuse University Press, 2001).

20   Julian Wolfreys, *Victorian Hauntings: Spectrality, Gothic, the Uncanny and Literature* (Basingstoke: Palgrave, 2002).

21   Anne Williams, *Art of Darkness: A Poetics of the Gothic* (Chicago: University of Chicago Press, 1995).

22   This book makes no differentiation between primary and secondary texts: all are treated as texts that comment upon the concepts under discussion.

23   Horace Walpole, *The Castle of Otranto* (Oxford: Oxford University Press, 1996 [1764]).

24   Derrida, 'Dissemination', in *Dissemination*.

25   Derrida, 'The double session', in *Dissemination*.

26   Derrida, 'Before the law', in Derek Attridge (ed.), *Acts of Literature* (London: Routledge, 1992).

27   Derrida, 'Force of law: the mystical foundation of authority', *Cardozo Law Review*, 11/5–6 (1990).

28   Derrida, 'Plato's pharmacy', in *Dissemination*.

29   Derrida, *Given Time: Counterfeit Money* (Chicago: University of Chicago Press, 1992).

Chapter 1

1   Mark Z. Danielewski, *House of Leaves* (London: Doubleday, 2000), p. xvii.

2   Will is referred to by his surname 'Navidson' throughout the text.

3   Danielewski, *House of Leaves*, p. 57.

4   His readings are described as explorations.

5   Not all of which are Zampanò.

6 Jacques Derrida, 'Plato's pharmacy', in *Dissemination* (London: Continuum, 2004 [1968]), p. 166.

7 Derrida, 'Plato's pharmacy', p. 167.

8 Catherine Spooner, *Contemporary Gothic* (London: Reaktion Books, 2006), p. 46.

9 Derrida, 'Différance', in *Margins of Philosophy* (Chicago: Harvester, 1982 [1972]), p. 4.

10 Derrida, 'Outwork, prefacing', in *Dissemination*, p. 9.

11 Barbara Johnson, 'Translator's introduction', in Derrida, *Dissemination*, p. ix.

12 Derrida, 'Différance', p. 11.

13 Ferdinand de Saussure, 'Course in general linguistics', in V. C. Leitch, *The Norton Anthology of Theory and Criticism* (London: Norton, 2001 [1916]), p. 976.

14 As logocentrism is aligned with patriarchal authority, the use of reason as a tool for mastery is clearly aligned with the masculine in *House of Leaves*.

15 Derrida, 'Différance', p. 6.

16 Ibid., p. 9.

17 Ibid., p. 23.

18 Ibid., p. 7.

19 Ibid., p. 3.

20 Derrida, *Of Grammatology* (London: The Johns Hopkins University Press, 1997 [1974]), p. 6.

21 Leitch, *The Norton Anthology of Theory and Criticism*, p. 1817.

22 Derrida, 'Freud and the scene of writing', in *Writing and Difference* (London: Routledge, 1978 [1967]), p. 280.

23 Derrida, 'Living on – Border lines', in Peggy Kamuf (ed.), *A Derrida Reader: Between the Blinds* (Hemel Hempstead: Harvester Wheatsheaf, 1991 [1979]), p. 257.

24 Derrida, 'Dissemination', in *Dissemination*, p. 368.

25 Derrida, 'Plato's pharmacy', p. 69.

26 Ibid., p. 69.

27 Derrida, 'Freud and the scene of writing', p. 278.

28 Derrida, *Of Grammatology*, p. 18.

29 As indicated by the etymology of the term 'Bible'.

30 Homi Bhabha, *The Location of Culture* (London: Routledge, 1994), p. 105.

31 Derrida, 'Plato's pharmacy', p. 102.

32 Ibid., p. 69.

33 A fictional reference.
34 Another fictional reference.
35 Derrida, 'Différance', p. 7.
36 Gayatri Chakravorty Spivak, 'Translator's preface', in Derrida, *Of Grammatology*, p. xiv.
37 Spooner, *Contemporary Gothic*, p. 43.
38 Derrida, *The Post Card: From Socrates to Freud and Beyond* (Chicago: University of Chicago Press, 1987), p. 11.
39 Catherine Malabou, *Counterpath: Traveling with Jacques Derrida* (Stanford, CA: Stanford University Press, 2004), p. 194.
40 Derrida, 'Outwork, prefacing', p. 3.
41 Derrida, 'Plato's pharmacy', p. 69.
42 Bhabha, *The Location of Culture*, p. 105.
43 Derrida, 'Dissemination', p. 377.
44 I am yet to meet a reader of *House of Leaves* who has not felt in some way consumed by it.
45 Derrida, 'Plato's pharmacy', p. 101.
46 Spooner, *Contemporary Gothic*, p. 46.

Chapter 2

1 Wandering without arrival is explored in more detail in chapter 1 in relation to the dissemination of signification.
2 Jacques Derrida, *The Post Card: From Socrates to Freud and Beyond* (Chicago: University of Chicago Press, 1987).
3 Catherine Malabou, *Counterpath: Traveling with Jacques Derrida* (Stanford, CA: Stanford University Press, 2004).
4 Malabou, *Counterpath*, pp. 16–18.
5 Ibid., p. 28.
6 The disseminative network of misinterpretation is considered further in chapter 1.
7 Malabou, *Counterpath*, p. 33.
8 Ibid., p. 4.
9 William Trevor, *The Story of Lucy Gault* (London: Penguin, 2002), p. 32.
10 Dislocated time is explored further in chapter 5 in relation to a skewed lineage that results in a perverse inheritance from father to son.
11 Trevor, *The Story of Lucy Gault*, p. 31.
12 Derrida, *The Post Card*, p. 79.

13 Ibid., p. 65.
14 Ibid., p. 35.
15 Ibid., p. 119.
16 The horror of child suicide is also discussed in chapter 3.
17 Malabou, *Counterpath*, p. 194.
18 Derrida, *The Post Card*, p. 33.
19 Sigmund Freud, 'The uncanny', in Albert Dickson (ed.), *Art and Literature* (London: Penguin, 1990 [1919]).
20 Fred Botting, *Gothic* (London: Routledge, 1995), p. 75.
21 Clive Bloom, 'Horror fiction: in search of a definition', in David Punter (ed.), *A Companion to the Gothic* (London: Blackwell, 2001), p. 164.
22 Bloom, 'Horror fiction: in search of a definition', p. 164.
23 Botting, *Gothic,* p. 10.
24 Roland Barthes, 'Myth today', in *Mythologies* (London: Paladin, 1973), p. 109.
25 Sandra Gilbert and Susan Gubar, *The Madwoman in the Attic: The Woman Writer and the Nineteenth-century Imagination* (London: Yale University Press, 2000).
26 Charlotte Brontë, *Jane Eyre* (London: Penguin, 1993 [1847]), p. 327.
27 Derrida, *The Post Card*, p. 51.
28 Ibid., p. 123.
29 Ibid., p. 29.
30 Ibid., p. 79.
31 Jacques Derrida and Elisabeth Roudinesco, *For what Tomorrow: A Dialogue* (Stanford, CA: Stanford University Press, 2004), p. 45.
32 Malabou, *Counterpath*, p. 40.
33 Ibid., p. 14.
34 Ibid., p. 14.
35 Derrida, *The Post Card*, p. 23.

Chapter 3

1 Jacques Derrida, 'The double session', in *Dissemination* (London: Continuum, 2004 [1970]), p. 221.
2 John Banville, *The Sea* (London: Picador, 2005), p. 24.
3 A rather different example of mourning is experienced by the protagonist under examination in chapter 4: the mourning of a lost sibling whose death forces an interaction with the law and hospitality.

4   Derrida, *Specters of Marx: The State of the Debt, the Work of Mourning, and the New International* (London: Routledge, 1994), p. 9.

5   Banville, *The Sea*, p. 237.

6   Julia Kristeva, *Black Sun: Depression and Melancholia* (New York: Columbia University Press, 1989), pp. 4–5.

7   Peter Goodrich, *Oedipus Lex: Psychoanalysis, History, Law* (Berkeley: University of California Press, 1995), p. 23.

8   Derrida, *Specters of Marx*, p. 129.

9   Derrida, 'The pit and the pyramid: introduction to Hegel's semiology', in *Margins of Philosophy* (Chicago: University of Chicago Press, 1982), p. 77.

10 Derrida, 'Plato's pharmacy', in *Dissemination* (London: Continuum, 2004 [1968]), p. 111.

11 Derrida, *Archive Fever: A Freudian Impression* (London: University of Chicago Press, 1989), p. 84.

12 Derrida, *Archive Fever*, p. 45.

13 The process of mourning as digestion and expulsion is explored further in chapter 4.

14 Sigmund Freud, 'Mourning and melancholia', in *General Psychological Theory: Papers on Metapsychology* (New York: Collier Books, 1963 [1917]), p. 166.

15 Kristeva, *Black Sun*, p. 60.

16 Freud, 'The uncanny', in Albert Dickson (ed.), *Art and Literature* (London: Penguin, 1990 [1919]).

17 René Girard, *Violence and the Sacred* (London: The Johns Hopkins University Press, 1972), p. 56.

18 Freud, 'The uncanny', p. 356.

19 Derrida, 'Plato's pharmacy', p. 111.

20 Derrida, *The Gift of Death* (Chicago: University of Chicago Press, 1996), p. 60.

21 Ibid., p. 60.

22 Emmanuel Levinas, *Totality and Infinity: An Essay on Exteriority* (The Hague and Boston: M. Nijhoff Publishers, 1979), p. 155.

23 Ibid., p. 43.

24 Ibid., p. 12.

25 Derrida, *The Gift of Death*, p. 68.

26 There is of course, an argument here for the gendered subject positions of Max and Chloe, as the role of the female can be understood as a vessel for the male sense of self. As discussed by feminists such as Luce Irigaray, woman has been read as the space of *différance*, a device for

masculine identity to be fulfilled. However, this viewpoint effectively cancels out the role of women and reduces them to a functional role. Such a position is not endorsed by the text through Chloe's dual role as twin.

27 Levinas, *Totality and Infinity*, p. 88.

28 Ibid., p. 43.

29 Mark Wigley, *The Architecture of Deconstruction: Derrida's Haunt* (London: MIT Press, 1993).

30 Levinas, *Totality and Infinity*, pp. 180–1.

31 Ibid., p. 233.

32 Kristeva, *Black Sun*, p. 167.

33 Like the protagonist in chapter 4, Max refuses to digest and expel through the legal process of mourning. However, unlike Veronica, Max incorporates the deceased other in his already dual sense of identity, whereas the other for Veronica is bound to her through duty and guilt, itself a re-invention of the other rather than a faithful memory.

34 Jacques Derrida and Elisabeth Roudinesco, *For what Tomorrow: A Dialogue* (Stanford, CA: Stanford University Press, 2004), p. 160.

35 Ibid., p. 160.

36 Georges Perec, *Species of Spaces and Other Pieces* (London: Penguin, 1997), p. 21.

37 Derrida, *Memoires for Paul de Man* (New York: Columbia University Press, 1986), p. 6.

38 Unlike Alison, the protagonist in chapter 6, Max cannot read traces of the dead, as he is not living in space but rather in the past. Due to this, he is not open to the other in mourning; he is lost within himself.

39 Derrida, *Archive Fever*, p. 111.

40 Ibid., p. 17.

41 Derrida, *Of Grammatology* (London: The Johns Hopkins University Press, 1997 [1974]), p. 151.

42 Susan Sontag, *On Photography* (London: Penguin, 2002 [1979]), p. 154.

43 Derrida, 'Ghost dance: an interview with Jacques Derrida', *Public*, 2 (1989), 61.

44 Barthes, Roland, *Camera Lucida* (London: Vintage Books, 1993), p. 21.

45 Ibid., p. 45.

46 Ibid., p. 53.

47 Ibid., pp. 56–7.

48 Ibid., p. 9.

49 Gideon Ofrat, *The Jewish Derrida* (Syracuse, NY: Syracuse University Press, 2001), p. 89.

50 Derrida, *Memoires for Paul de Man*, p. 58.

51 Derrida, *Of Grammatology*, p. 70.

52 Derrida, 'The double session', p. 212.

53 Ibid., p. 214.

54 Ibid., p. 221.

55 Ibid., p. 221.

56 Kristeva, *Black Sun*, p. 4.

57 Freud, 'Mourning and melancholia', p. 165.

58 Derrida, *Adieu to Emmanuel Levinas* (Stanford, CA: Stanford University Press, 1997), p. 6.

59 Derrida, *Specters of Marx*, p. 133.

60 The significance of the will is examined in more detail in chapter 5.

61 Derrida, *Memoires for Paul de Man*, p. 60.

62 Kristeva, *Black Sun*, p. 12.

63 Derrida, *Politics of Friendship* (London: Verso Books, 1997), p. 122.

64 Derrida, *Specters of Marx*, xviii.

Chapter 4

1 Anne Enright, *The Gathering* (London: Jonathan Cape, 2007), p. 42.

2 Jacques Derrida and Elisabeth Roudinesco, *For what Tomorrow: A Dialogue* (Stanford, CA: Stanford University Press, 2004), p. 159.

3 Today, suicide is a religious transgression (particularly in Catholicism), but no longer against the law.

4 Enright, *The Gathering*, p. 10.

5 Derrida, 'Before the law', in Derek Attridge (ed.), *Acts of Literature* (London: Routledge, 1992), p. 206.

6 Julia Kristeva, 'Powers of horror: an essay on abjection', in Kelly Oliver, *The Portable Kristeva* (New York: Columbia University Press, 1997 [1982]), p. 232.

7 Mark Wigley, *The Architecture of Deconstruction: Derrida's Haunt* (London: MIT Press, 1993), p. 149.

8 Derrida, *The Ear of the Other: Texts and Discussions with Jacques Derrida* (London: University of Nebraska Press, 1988), p. 7.

9 Wigley, *The Architecture of Deconstruction*, p. 150.

10 The posthumous control of the law is also examined in chapter 6 in relation to mortgage, a binding of the law to subjects alive and dead.

11 Derrida, 'Freud and the scene of writing', in *Writing and Difference* (London:

Routledge, 1978 [1967]), p. 197.

12 Derrida, *Acts of Religion* (London: Routledge, 2002), p. 242.

13 Gideon Ofrat, *The Jewish Derrida* (Syracuse, NY: Syracuse University Press, 2001), p. 78.

14 Peter Goodrich, *Oedipus Lex: Psychoanalysis, History, Law* (Berkeley: University of California Press, 1995), p. 41.

15 Derrida, 'Before the law', p. 191.

16 Ibid., p. 205.

17 Ibid., p. 208.

18 Ibid., p. 199.

19 Goodrich, *Oedipus Lex*, p. 8.

20 The spectrality of currency is discussed further in chapter 6.

21 Derrida, *Paper Machine* (Stanford, CA: Stanford University Press, 2005), p. 58.

22 Ibid., p. 6.

23 Derrida, 'Freud and the scene of writing', p. 223.

24 Derrida, *Paper Machine*, p. 56.

25 Ofrat, *The Jewish Derrida*, p. 87.

26 Goodrich, *Oedipus Lex*.

27 Derrida, 'Force of law: the mystical foundation of authority', *Cardozo Law Review*, 11/5–6 (1990), 997.

28 Wigley, *The Architecture of Deconstruction*, p. 43.

29 Ibid., p. 128.

30 Ofrat, *The Jewish Derrida*, p. 122.

31 Derrida, *The Gift of Death* (Chicago: University of Chicago Press, 1996), p. 31.

32 Derrida, *Of Hospitality: Anne Dufourmantelle invites Jacques Derrida to Respond* (Stanford, CA: Stanford University Press, 2000), p. 157.

33 Derrida, *Acts of Religion*, p. 364.

34 Derrida, *Of Hospitality*, p. 107.

35 Ibid., p. 123.

36 Derrida, *Paper Machine*, p. 66.

37 Derrida, *Of Hospitality*, p. 25.

38 Kristeva, 'Powers of horror', p. 232.

39 As explored in chapter 6, the ghost becomes a simultaneously legal and illegal subject, both within the law and outside it.

40 Goodrich, *Oedipus Lex*, p. 94.

41 Derrida, *Of Hospitality*, pp. 150–2.

42 Ibid., p. 61.

43 Goodrich, *Oedipus Lex*, pp. 10–11.

44 Ibid., p. 131.

45 The relation of father to son is examined in more detail in chapter 5.

46 Derrida, *Paper Machine*, p. 116.

47 Derrida, *Specters of Marx: The State of the Debt, the Work of Mourning, and the New International* (London: Routledge, 1994), p. 101.

48 It is not clear in the text if Veronica's grandmother, Ada, is aware of the abuse of her grandson.

49 Jacques Derrida and Maurizio Ferraris, *A Taste for the Secret* (Malden, MA: Polity Press, 2001), p. 7.

50 Derrida, 'Force of law', p. 935.

51 Ibid., p. 961.

52 The horror of the unspeakable is also explored in chapter 2.

53 Veronica's architectural experience of mourning is aligned with her occupation as an interior designer.

54 Textual ownership achieved through the law is examined in chapter 3 alongside a discussion of profit through the financing of mortgage.

55 Kristeva, 'Powers of horror', p. 231.

56 Michel Foucault, *Birth of the Clinic* (London: Routledge, 1993 [1973]), p. 39.

57 Ofrat, *The Jewish Derrida*, p. 60.

58 Derrida, 'The pit and the pyramid: introduction to Hegel's semiology', in *Margins of Philosophy* (Chicago: University of Chicago Press, 1982), p. 130.

59 Wigley, *The Architecture of Deconstruction*, p. 82.

60 Ibid., p. 9.

61 Kristeva, 'Powers of horror', p. 243.

62 Derrida, *Specters of Marx*, p. 40.

63 Ibid., p. 41.

64 Wigley, *The Architecture of Deconstruction*, p. 127.

65 Ibid., p. 137.

66 Derrida, *Limited Inc* (Evanston, IL: Northwestern University Press, 1988), p. 90.

67 Wigley, *The Architecture of Deconstruction*, pp. 125–6.

68 Goodrich, *Oedipus Lex*, p. 19.

69 Ibid., p. 19.

70 Derrida, *The Ear of the Other*, pp. 57–8.

71 Wigley, *The Architecture of Deconstruction*, p. 144.

72 Ibid., p. 131.

73 Goodrich, *Oedipus Lex*, p. 39.

74 Such a refusal can be aligned with Bret, the protagonist in chapter 5, who initially ignores the demands of his father's ghost.

75 Wigley, *The Architecture of Deconstruction*, p. 144.

Chapter 5

1   Unlike other chapters, the phrase 'out of joint' is enclosed in quotation marks here as this is a direct quotation from both *Hamlet* and *Specters of Marx*, which are explored throughout chapter 5. The phrase a time 'out of joint' comes from *Hamlet*, II/i, 186, and also figures as the epigraph to *Specters of Marx*.

2   Jacques Derrida, *Of Grammatology* (London: The Johns Hopkins University Press, 1997 [1974]), p. 158.

3   Jacques Derrida and Elisabeth Roudinesco, *For what Tomorrow: A Dialogue* (Stanford, CA: Stanford University Press, 2004), p. 2.

4   The dissemination of signification is explored further in chapter 1.

5   Derrida, *Specters of Marx: The State of the Debt, the Work of Mourning, and the New International* (London: Routledge, 1994), p. 20.

6   Bret Easton Ellis, *Lunar Park* (London: Picador, 2005), p. 253.

7   Derrida, 'Plato's pharmacy', in *Dissemination* (London: Continuum, 2004 [1968]), p. 146.

8   Easton Ellis, *Lunar Park*, p. 77.

9   William Shakespeare, *Hamlet*, ed. Neil Taylor and Anne Thomson (London: Arden Shakespeare, Thomson Learning, 2006), I/v, 98.

10   *Hamlet*, III/i, 149.

11   Horace Walpole, *The Castle of Otranto* (Oxford: Oxford University Press, 1996 [1764]), pp. 10–11.

12   Walpole, *The Castle of Otranto*, p. 112.

13   Ibid., p. 115.

14   *Hamlet*, I/ii, 89–92.

15   Ibid., II/i, 186.

16   Anne Williams, *Art of Darkness: A Poetics of the Gothic* (Chicago: University of Chicago Press, 1995), p. 31.

17   Walpole, *The Castle of Otranto*, p. 113.

18   *Hamlet*, V/ii, 63.

19   Derrida, 'Plato's pharmacy', p. 152.

20   Julian Wolfreys, *Victorian Hauntings: Spectrality, Gothic, the Uncanny and Literature* (Basingstoke: Palgrave, 2002), p. 5.

21   As explored in 'Plato's pharmacy', Derrida alludes to the multiple translations of the Greek word *pharmakon*. Amongst these are the somewhat contradictory positions of 'poison' or 'remedy', and 'cure' or 'medicine'. In this chapter, the term is aligned with the simultaneity of the father's presence: both cure (in his attempt to remedy his dislocated inheritance) and poison (evident through the destructive events induced by his spectre).

22   *Hamlet*, I/v, 61.

23 Derrida, 'Plato's pharmacy', p. 120.
24 *Hamlet*, V/ii, 312.
25 Ibid., V/ii, 315.
26 Ibid., V/ii, 306.
27 Ibid., V/ii, 281.
28 Ibid., V/ii, 320.
29 Derrida, 'Plato's pharmacy', p. 150.
30 Walpole, *The Castle of Otranto*, p. 57.
31 Derrida, *Specters of Marx*, p. 7.
32 Ibid., p. 9.
33 Jacques Derrida and Elisabeth Roudinesco, *For what Tomorrow*, p. 6.
34 *Hamlet*, III/i, 55.
35 Derrida, 'Plato's pharmacy', p. 153.
36 Ibid., p. 75.
37 *Hamlet*, I/iv, 75.
38 Walpole, *The Castle of Otranto*, p. 109.
39 As inherited from his father.
40 Walpole, *The Castle of Otranto*, p. 115.

Chapter 6

1 As explored in chapter 4.
2 Hilary Mantel, *Beyond Black* (London: Harper Perennial, 2005), p. 6.
3 Jacques Derrida, *Specters of Marx: The State of the Debt, the Work of Mourning, and the New International* (London: Routledge, 1994), p. 45.
4 Derrida, *Specters of Marx*, p. 214.
5 Derrida, *Given Time: Counterfeit Money* (Chicago: University of Chicago Press, 1992), p. 216.
6 Derrida, *Specters of Marx*, p. 45.
7 Mantel, *Beyond Black*, p. 200.
8 Derrida, *Given Time*, p. 7.
9 Derrida, *The Ear of the Other: Texts and Discussions with Jacques Derrida* (London: University of Nebraska Press, 1988), p. 7.
10 Derrida, *Specters of Marx*, p. 46.
11 Ibid., p. 42.
12 Georges Perec, *Species of Spaces and Other Pieces* (London: Penguin, 1997), p. 15.
13 Mark Wigley, *The Architecture of Deconstruction: Derrida's Haunt* (London: MIT Press, 1993), p. 109.

14   Gatherings of spectres and mourners are explored in more detail in chapter 4.

15   Derrida, *Specters of Marx*, p. 3.

16   Wigley, *The Architecture of Deconstruction*, p. 156.

17   John R. Stilgoe, 'Introduction', in Gaston Bachelard, *The Poetics of Space* (Boston: Beacon Press, 1994 [1958]), vii.

18   Derrida, *Specters of Marx*, p. 109.

19   Carolyn Steedman, *Dust* (Manchester: Manchester University Press, 2001), p. 17.

20   Wigley, *The Architecture of Deconstruction*, p. 120.

21   Steedman, *Dust*, p. 19.

22   Ibid., p. 76.

23   Derrida, 'Force of law: the mystical foundation of authority', *Cardozo Law Review*, 11/5–6 (1990), 943.

24   Wigley, *The Architecture of Deconstruction*, p. 147.

25   Derrida, *Specters of Marx*, p. 108.

26   Ibid., p. 109.

27   Wigley, *The Architecture of Deconstruction*, p. 114.

28   Derrida, *Specters of Marx*, p. 109.

29   Disjointed lineage is explored in more detail in chapter 5 in relation to *Hamlet*. The haunting of the son by the father means that the son must submit to the patriarchal law of the father. The theme of lineage permeates this book as a haunting demand (in the case of the father) and a spectral absence (in the desire for a descendant).

30   Derrida, *Paper Machine* (Stanford, CA: Stanford University Press, 2005), p. 44.

31   Derrida, *Specters of Marx*, p. 45.

32   Peter Goodrich, *Oedipus Lex: Psychoanalysis, History, Law* (Berkeley: University of California Press, 1995), p. 42.

33   Derrida, *Paper Machine*, p. 2.

34   Derrida, *Given Time: Counterfeit Money*, p. 134.

35   Wigley, *The Architecture of Deconstruction*, p. 160.

36   In Lee Kovacs, *The Haunted Screen: Ghosts in Literature and Film* (London: McFarland, 1999), p. 4.

37   Steedman, *Dust*, p. 76.

38   Derrida, *Learning to Live Finally: The Last Interview* (New Jersey: Melville House Publishing, 2007), p. 14.

Afterword

1 Simon Critchley, *Very Little . . . Almost Nothing* (London: Routledge, 2004), p. 171.

2 Bret Easton Ellis, *American Psycho* (London: Picador, 1991), p. 384.

Bibliography

Bachelard, Gaston, 'Introduction', in *The Poetics of Space* (Boston: Beacon Press, 1994 [1958]), xv–xxxix.

Banville, John, *The Sea* (London: Picador, 2005).

Barthes, Roland, 'Myth today', in *Mythologies*, trans. A. Lavers (London: Paladin, 1973), pp. 131–59.

——, *Camera Lucida*, trans. R. Howard (London: Vintage Books, 1993).

Bhabha, Homi, *The Location of Culture* (London: Routledge, 1994).

Bloom, Clive, 'Horror fiction: in search of a definition', in David Punter (ed.), *A Companion to the Gothic* (London: Blackwell, 2001), pp. 155–66.

Botting, Fred, *Gothic* (London: Routledge, 1995).

Brontë, Charlotte, *Jane Eyre* (London: Penguin, 1993 [1847]).

Castricano, Jodey, *Cryptomimesis: The Gothic and Jacques Derrida's Ghost Writing* (London: McGill-Queen's University Press, 2001).

Critchley, Simon, *Very Little . . . Almost Nothing* (London: Routledge, 2004).

Danielewski, Mark Z., *House of Leaves* (London: Doubleday, 2000).

Derrida, Jacques, 'Freud and the scene of writing', in *Writing and Difference*, trans. A. Bass (London: Routledge, 1978 [1967]), pp. 196–231.

——, 'Plato's pharmacy', in *Dissemination*, trans. B. Johnson (London: Continuum, 2004 [1968]), pp. 67–154.

——, 'Dissemination', in *Dissemination* [1969], pp. 317–93.

——, 'The double session', in *Dissemination* [1970], pp. 187–316.

——, 'Différance', in *Margins of Philosophy*, trans. A. Bass (Chicago: Harvester, 1982 [1972]), pp. 3–27.

——, *Of Grammatology*, trans. G. C. Spivak (London: The Johns Hopkins University Press, 1997 [1974]).

——, 'Living on – Border lines', in Peggy Kamuf (ed.), *A Derrida Reader: Between the Blinds* (Hemel Hempstead: Harvester Wheatsheaf, 1991 [1979]), pp. 257–68.

——, 'Outwork, prefacing', in *Dissemination* [1981], pp. 1–66.

——, *Margins of Philosophy*, trans. A. Bass (Chicago: University of Chicago Press, 1982).

——, 'The pit and the pyramid: introduction to Hegel's semiology', in *Margins of Philosophy*, pp. 69–108.

——, *Memoires for Paul de Man*, trans. E. Cadava, J. Culler and C. Lindsay (New York: Columbia University Press, 1986).

——, *The Post Card: From Socrates to Freud and Beyond*, trans. A. Bass (Chicago: University of Chicago Press, 1987).

——, *The Ear of the Other: Texts and Discussions with Jacques Derrida*, trans. P. Kamuf (London: University of Nebraska Press, 1988).

——, *Archive Fever: A Freudian Impression*, trans. E. Prenowitz (London: University of Chicago Press, 1989).

——, 'Ghost dance: an interview with Jacques Derrida', *Public*, 2 (1989), 60–7.

——, 'Force of law: the mystical foundation of authority', *Cardozo Law Review*, 11/5–6 (1990), 920–1045.

——, 'Before the law', in Derek Attridge (ed.), *Acts of Literature* (London: Routledge, 1992), pp. 183–220.

——, *Given Time: Counterfeit Money*, trans. P. Kamuf (Chicago: University of Chicago Press, 1992).

——, *Specters of Marx: The State of the Debt, the Work of Mourning, and the New International*, trans. P. Kamuf (London: Routledge, 1994).

——, *The Gift of Death*, trans. D. Wills (Chicago: University of Chicago Press, 1996).

——, *Adieu to Emmanuel Levinas*, trans. P. Brault and M. Naas (Stanford, CA: Stanford University Press, 1997).

——, *Politics of Friendship*, trans. G. Collins (London: Verso Books, 1997).

——, *Of Hospitality: Anne Dufourmantelle invites Jacques Derrida to Respond*, trans. R. Bowlby (Stanford, CA: Stanford University Press, 2000).

——, *Acts of Religion*, trans. G. Anidjar (London: Routledge, 2002).

——, *Paper Machine*, trans. R. Bowlby (Stanford, CA: Stanford University Press, 2005).

—— and Maurizio Ferraris, *A Taste for the Secret*, trans. G. Donis (Malden, MA: Polity Press, 2001).

—— and Elisabeth Roudinesco, *For what Tomorrow: A Dialogue*, trans. J. Fort (Stanford, CA: Stanford University Press, 2004).

Easton Ellis, Bret, *American Psycho* (London: Picador, 1991).

——, *Lunar Park* (London: Picador, 2005).

Enright, Anne, *The Gathering* (London: Jonathan Cape, 2007).

Foucault, Michel, *Birth of the Clinic* (London: Routledge, 1993 [1973]).

Freud, Sigmund, 'Mourning and melancholia', in *General Psychological Theory: Papers on Metapsychology* (New York: Collier Books, 1963 [1917]), pp. 164–79.

——, 'The uncanny', in Albert Dickson (ed.), *Art and Literature* (London: Penguin, 1990 [1919]), pp. 339–76.

Gilbert, Sandra and Susan Gubar, *The Madwoman in the Attic: The Woman Writer and the Nineteenth-century Imagination* (London: Yale University Press, 2000).

Girard, René, *Violence and the Sacred* (London: The Johns Hopkins University Press, 1972).

Goodrich, Peter, *Oedipus Lex: Psychoanalysis, History, Law* (Berkeley: University of California Press, 1995).

Johnson, Barbara, 'Translator's introduction', in Derrida, *Dissemination*, vii–xxxv.

Kristeva, Julia, 'Powers of horror: an essay on abjection', in Kelly Oliver, *The Portable Kristeva* (New York: Columbia University Press, 1997 [1982]), pp. 229–63.

——, *Black Sun: Depression and Melancholia*, trans. L. Roudiez (New York: Columbia University Press, 1989).

Leitch, V. C., *The Norton Anthology of Theory and Criticism* (London: Norton, 2001).

Levinas, Emmanuel, *Totality and Infinity: An Essay on Exteriority*, trans. A. Lingis (The Hague and Boston: M. Nijhoff Publishers, 1979).

Malabou, Catherine, *Counterpath: Traveling with Jacques Derrida* (Stanford, CA: Stanford University Press, 2004).

Mantel, Hilary, *Beyond Black* (London: Harper Perennial, 2005).

Ofrat, Gideon, *The Jewish Derrida* (Syracuse, NY: Syracuse University Press, 2001).

Perec, Georges, *Species of Spaces and Other Pieces* (London: Penguin, 1997).

Poe, Edgar Allen, *The Masque of the Red Death and other stories* (London: Penguin, 2008 [1842]).

Punter, David, 'The ghost of a history', in D. Punter (ed.), *A Companion to the Gothic* (London: Blackwell, 2001), vii–xiv.

Royle, Nicholas, *In Memory of Jacques Derrida* (Edinburgh: Edinburgh University Press, 2009).

Saussure, Ferdinand de, 'Course in general linguistics', in Leitch, *The Norton Anthology of Theory and Criticism* [1916], pp. 960–77.

Sontag, Susan, *On Photography* (London: Penguin, 2002 [1979]).

Spivak, Gayatri Chakravorty, 'Translator's preface', in Derrida, *Of Grammatology*, ix–lxxxvii.

Spooner, Catherine, *Contemporary Gothic* (London: Reaktion Books, 2006).

——, 'Introduction: Gothic in contemporary popular culture', *Gothic Studies*, 9/1 (2007), 1–4.

Steedman, Carolyn, *Dust* (Manchester: Manchester University Press, 2001).

Taylor, Neil and Anne Thomson (eds), *Hamlet* (London: Arden Shakespeare, Thomson Learning, 2006).

Trevor, William, *The Story of Lucy Gault* (London: Penguin, 2002).

Walpole, Horace, *The Castle of Otranto* (Oxford: Oxford University Press, 1996 [1764]).

Warwick, Alex, 'Feeling Gothicky?', *Gothic Studies*, 9/1 (2007), 5–15.

Williams, Anne, *Art of Darkness: A Poetics of the Gothic* (Chicago: University of Chicago Press, 1995).

Wigley, Mark, *The Architecture of Deconstruction: Derrida's Haunt* (London: MIT Press, 1993).

Wild, John, 'Introduction', in Levinas, *Totality and Infinity*, pp. 1–20.

Wolfreys, Julian, *Victorian Hauntings: Spectrality, Gothic, the Uncanny and Literature* (Basingstoke: Palgrave, 2002).

Index

ॐ